BY THE EDITORS OF CONSUMER GUIDE®

Appliance Repairs
Made Easy

Contents

Printed and bound by Graficki Zavod Hrvatske & Printing House Founded 1874

   3 4 5 6 7 8 9 10

Library of Congress Catalog Card Number: 80-81973

Cover Design: Frank E. Peiler
Cover Photography: Mel Winer
Illustrations: Clarence A. Moberg
Acknowledgment: The Editors of Consumer Guide® wish to thank National Supply, of Wheeling, Illinois, for allowing us to photograph some of their products.

Basic Appliance Repair Principles

Like all the conveniences of modern living, appliances have become not a luxury but a necessity. Major appliances provide comfort and convenience; they keep your home working smoothly and efficiently; they save time and trouble and work. They don't make up a single system, but together they act as one of the most important components of your home: the service-providers, the mechanical gadgets that do the drudge work and simplify all your housekeeping chores.

Appliances are built to perform. They work hard, year after year—and, usually, without too many problems. They're easy to take for granted. The result is that when an appliance breaks down, you may be completely at a loss—you don't know how it works or why it's stopped working, much less how to fix it. In this situation, you're at the mercy of the professionals — and professional repair services are expensive.

Actually, appliances are not anything you should be afraid of. All appliances work on the same fundamental principles, and all appliance repairs are based on these principles. When you know the basic maintenance and repair procedures, you can keep your appliances working right, and take care of almost all repair jobs.

HOW APPLIANCES WORK

Most appliances operate on your home's electrical system; they use AC current from the circuit wiring in your home. Small appliances work on 110-120-volt circuits; the plugs on their cords have two blades. Large appliances, such as air conditioners, dryers, and ranges, usually require 220-240-volt wiring, and cannot be operated on 110-120-volt circuits. Large appliances are wired with a grounding wire; their plugs have two blades and a prong. This type of appliance must be plugged into a grounded outlet—one with openings to accept both blades and grounding prong—or grounded with a special adapter plug. All appliances are labeled, either on a metal plate or on the appliance casing, to show their power requirements in watts and volts, and sometimes in amps. When you buy an appliance, re-member that the higher its power requirements are, the more electricity it will use, and the more it will cost to operate.

Small appliances are usually fairly simple machines. They may consist of a simple heating element, or of a fan, a set of blades, or rotating beaters attached to a drive shaft; or they may have two or three simple mechanical linkages. Repairs to these appliances are usually correspondingly simple. Large appliances are more complex — one major appliance, such as a washing machine, may have a motor, a timer, a pump, and various valves, switches, and solenoids. In this type of appliance, problems can occur in either the control devices or the mechanical/power components. Failure of a control device may affect one operation or the entire appliance; failure of a mechanical/power device usually affects only the functions that depend on that device. When a large appliance breaks down, knowing how to diagnose the problem is as important as knowing how to fix it.

Because large appliances are so complex, it usually isn't obvious where a malfunction is. The first step is to decide whether the problem is in a control device or a mechanical device. In a dryer, for example, the control devices govern the heat; the mechanical components turn the drum. Which system is affected? If the drum turns but the dryer doesn't heat, the problem is in the control system; if the dryer heats but the drum doesn't turn, the problem is mechanical. This kind of analysis can be used to pinpoint the type of failure — control system or mechanical system—in all large appliances.

To find out exactly what the problem is, you must check each part of the affected system to find the malfunctioning part. This isn't as difficult as it sounds, because appliance components work together in a logical sequence; starting with the simplest possibilities, you can test the components one by one to isolate the cause of the failure. The troubleshooting charts in this chapter will help you diagnose the problem. Each chart also describes the measures you should take to repair the appliance once you've found the problem.

KEY APPLIANCE REPAIR PRINCIPLES

There are three very important rules to follow in making appliance repairs:

• *Always* — with no exceptions — make sure the electric power and/or the gas supply to the appliance is disconnected *before* you test the appliance to diagnose the problem, or make any repairs. If you turn the power on to check your work after making a repair, do not touch the appliance; just turn the power on and observe. Never touch the appliance while it is running. If adjustments are needed, turn the power off before you make them.

• If the parts of an appliance are held together with screws, bolts, plugs, and other take-apart fasteners, you can probably make any necessary repairs. If the parts are held together with rivets or welds, don't try to repair the appliance yourself; call a professional service person.

• In most cases, broken or malfunctioning appliance parts can be replaced more quickly and inexpensively than they could be repaired, by you or by a professional. Replace broken or malfunctioning parts with new parts made especially for the appliance. Appliance parts are available from appliance service centers, appliance repair dealers, and appliance parts stores. You don't *always* have to go to a specific brand-name appliance parts service center to obtain the parts and service you need for brand-name appliances, so you have some shopping/service choice. If you can't locate a parts service center in your area, order the part you need directly from the manufacturer; give the manufacturer all the model and parts data possible for the appliance. The name and address of the appliance manufacturer are usually printed on the appliance.

These three basics are essential for safe and successful appliance repairs. Don't ever try to save time or money by ignoring them — you won't save anything at all, and you could end up hurting yourself or ruining the appliance.

Before you make any appliance repair, make sure the appliance is receiving power — lack of power is the most common cause of appliance failure. Before you start the testing and diagnosis process, take these preliminary steps:

• Check to make sure that the appliance is properly and firmly plugged in, and that the cord, the plug, and the outlet are working properly. If the outlet is controlled by a switch, make sure the switch is turned on. To determine whether an outlet is working, test it with a voltage tester, as detailed below in the section on electrical testing.

• Check to make sure the fuses and/or circuit breakers that control the circuit have not blown or trip-

ped. There may be more than one electrical entrance panel for your home, especially for 220-240-volt appliances such as ranges and air conditioners — check for blown fuses or tripped circuit breakers at both the main panel and the separate panel. If necessary, restore the circuit.

• Check to make sure fuses and/or breakers *in the appliance* are not blown or tripped. Push the reset buttons on such appliances as garbage disposers, washers, dryers, and ranges. Some ranges have separate plug-type fuses for oven operation; make sure these fuses have not blown.

• If the appliance uses gas or water, check to make sure it is receiving an adequate supply.

• Check your owner's manual; many manufacturers include very helpful problem/solution troubleshooting charts. If you don't have a manual for an appliance, you can probably get one — even for an old or obsolete appliance — from the manufacturer's customer service department.

Disassembling and Reassembling Appliances

Before you can repair an appliance, you'll almost always have to disassemble it to some extent. All appliances are different, but the disassembly procedure is always the same: basically, you must remove the parts in reverse of the way the manufacturer put them together. Remember that you'll have to put the appliance back together again. Lay the parts out in order as you

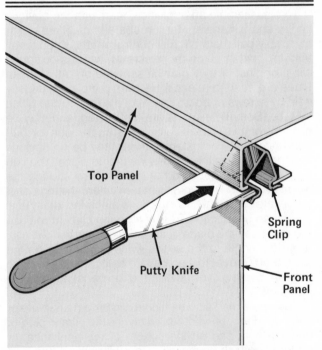

Spring clips are often hidden. To remove the top of a washing machine, for instance, use a putty knife to find the clip; then push in against it to release the top.

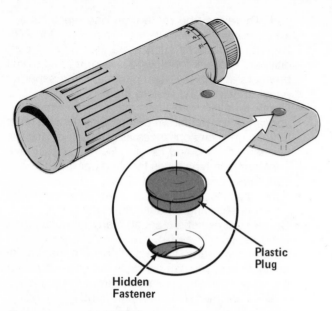

Fasteners are often hidden beneath a scarcely visible plastic plug. To disassemble the appliance, carefully pry up the plug to expose the fastener.

remove them, with fasteners at hand. If you aren't sure you'll be able to put the appliance back together, take notes and make drawings as you work. Label all terminals and wires if you must disconnect more than one wire at a time. Check your owner's manual for assembly diagrams and instructions.

To disassemble an appliance, start with the obvious knobs and fasteners. Many knobs and dials are push-fit; simply pull them off their control shafts. Knobs may also be held in place by setscrews, springs or spring clips, or pins; or they may be screwed on. All of these types are easy to release. Housing panels are usually held by screws or bolts; they may also be held in place by tabs. Sometimes parts are force-fitted, and may be hard to remove. Never force parts apart; look for hidden fasteners. For instance, there may be no obvious fasteners holding the top of a washer in place. You can locate the clips that hold the top down by sticking the blade of a putty knife into the seam where the top panel meets the side panel; run the knife along the seam until you hit an obstruction. This is a spring clip. To release the clip, push the blade of the knife directly into the clip, at a right angle to the seam, while pushing up on the top panel. Repeat this procedure to locate and remove any other spring clips holding the top panel; then lift the panel off.

Fasteners may also be hidden under a nameplate or company logo, behind a scarcely visible plastic plug or under a cork pad on the bottom of the appliance, or under an attachment plate. Carefully pry up the part that's hiding the fastener. When you reassemble the appliance, snap the concealing part back over the fas-

tener, or, if necessary, glue it into place. If you can't find hidden fasteners on force-fitted parts, warm the parts gently with a heating pad; the heat may make disassembly easier. Inside the appliance, watch for clips holding parts to the housing panels.

After making the repair, and before reassembling the appliance, vacuum inside the appliance to remove all dust and lint. Check for other problems and make any necessary repairs or adjustments. If the appliance has a motor, lubricate the motor; check carbon brushes in universal motors for wear, and replace them if necessary, as detailed below in the section on motor maintenance and repairs. Lubricate moving parts sparingly, and make sure electrical contacts are clean.

Reassemble the appliance in reverse of the way you took it apart; never force parts together or overtighten fasteners. Make sure moving parts, such as armatures or gears, don't bind. After reassembly, connect the appliance and turn it on. If it makes noise, smells, or overheats, turn it off and disconnect the power. Then go back over your repair to see where the problem is.

MECHANICAL AND ELECTRICAL SAFETY

You may be tempted to work on an appliance while it's running, or to test an appliance while the power is on. This is something you can never do safely. *Never* work on any running appliance that's had its access or service panels removed; *never* stick your hands or your tools into moving parts such as gears, belts, pulleys, and other moving components. When you turn the power on to check your work after making a repair, *do not* touch the appliance; simply turn the power on and observe. If adjustments are needed, turn the power off before you make them.

There's one more very important safety factor to remember in making appliance repairs: electricity can be dangerous, and you should *never* allow yourself or your tools to make contact with an electrical current. You must be extremely careful when making repairs to appliances powered by electricity. Before you start work on an appliance, unplug it from its power source. If it can't be unplugged, turn off the power to the circuit that supplies electricity to the appliance by removing the fuse or tripping the circuit breaker to the circuit at the main entrance panel in your home, or, in some cases, at a separate entrance panel. After turning off the power, test the appliance to make sure it's off. If the appliance doesn't work, *do not* assume that the power is off. Instead, check the leads to a motor, convenience light, or other component of the appliance that can be tested with a voltage tester. If the light of the tester does not come on, you can assume that the electricity to the appliance is off. If it does come on, the appliance is still connected, and you must locate the power source and turn it off before proceeding further.

Large appliances often have electrical circuits separate from the main power panel. This is especially true in older homes where appliances such as washers, dryers, ranges, and air conditioners have been added after the original wiring was done. Because large appliances require more power than many old wiring systems can supply, a separate fuse or circuit-breaker system is sometimes installed to handle the extra electrical load. These auxiliary power entrances are usually — but not always — located near the main entrance panel. Make a thorough check for additional entrance boxes before you assume the power is off.

Grounding Systems. Most stationary appliances (washers, dryers, ranges) are grounded by a wire that's attached to a cold-water pipe. The cold-water pipe runs into the ground outside your home, and thus grounds the appliance so that any leaking electricity goes into the ground. Disconnect this grounding wire before you make repairs, and be sure to reconnect it before you turn the power back on.

Many homes today are equipped with electrical outlets with a three-wire system. The third wire is a grounding device, and operates the same way as the grounding wire on stationary appliances. Large appliances, whose plugs have two blades and a prong, should be plugged into a grounded outlet, or grounded with a special adapter plug. *Caution: Never remove the prong from a three-wire plug to make it fit an ungrounded outlet; always use an adapter plug.*

Proper grounding is vital for metal-framed appliances. If the insulation on the power cord of a metal-framed appliance (such as a washer or dryer) is broken or worn away just at the point where the cord enters the frame, contact between the current conductor and the metal frame could charge the whole appliance with electricity—obviously a dangerous situation. When this happens, even if the appliance is properly grounded, dampness can cause a shock hazard. If you touched a charged metal frame in a damp location, or while touching a water faucet or radiator, the current would surge through you, and could kill you.

There are three things you can do to eliminate this hazard. First, make sure your appliances are properly grounded. Second, make sure that appliance cords are in good repair, and that they are not chafing against burrs or rough spots where they enter the appliance frame. And third, add a ground-fault circuit interrupter (GFI or GFCI) to the circuit. Ground-fault circuit interrupters are monitoring devices that instantly shut off a circuit when a current leak occurs; they are required by the National Electrical Code on all new 15- and 20-amp outdoor outlets, and for wiring in bathrooms, where dampness is a common problem. GFIs are available to plug into existing outlets as adapters, to replace outlets, and to replace circuit breakers in the electrical entrance panel. A professional electrician should install the circuit-breaker type; you can install the other types yourself. Ground-fault circuit interrupters are available at electrical supply and home center stores.

BASIC TOOLS: THE APPLIANCE REPAIR WORKSHOP

For most appliance repair jobs, you'll need only simple tools, both mechanical and electrical. These tools are inexpensive, readily available, and easy to use; you may well have most of them in your workshop already. There is some very sophisticated equipment needed for complex repair work, and this equipment is expensive—but it's still, in the long run, less expensive than professional service. For most jobs, however, simple tools are adequate.

Buy your appliance repair tools as you need them, if you don't already own these basics. The necessities are simple. First, you'll need a selection of good-quality screwdrivers—at least three sizes for standard slotted screws, and at least one Phillips-type screwdriver. A long-nosed pliers is essential. You'll also need a hammer—a claw hammer is fine—an adjustable wrench and a socket wrench set, a pump-type oil can, a utility knife, and a trouble light. Some simple electrical equipment is also necessary—a fuse puller, a multi-purpose tool for stripping the insulation off conductors and crimping solderless connectors, a test wire or jumper wire with an alligator clip on each end, and a 20,000-ohm, 2-watt wire-wound resistor, for work on capacitor-type motors. Resistors are not expensive; they're available at most appliance and television parts stores. All of your electrical tools should have insulated handles.

For work on small appliances, you'll need the same tools; you'll also need some smaller screwdrivers. A circlip pliers, for removing the retaining clip on some gear assemblies, is handy but not absolutely necessary; a screwdriver will often serve the same purpose. Materials needed for work on small appliances include heat-resistant oil, made for use in heat-producing appliances; silicone gear grease, available at appliance repair outlets; and electrical contact cleaner, available at appliance repair and electrical supply outlets. You'll also need fine emery boards and very fine (No. 0000) steel wool for cleaning electrical contacts, and a good supply of clean, soft cloths.

Tools for Electrical Testing

Many appliance repairs also require electrical testing for accurate diagnosis of the problem. At least 80 percent of the time, you'll be able to pinpoint an appliance malfunction from the troubleshooting charts included in this chapter, and proceed from them to make the repair. But the other 20 percent of the time, you'll need one of three electrical testing devices to spot the problem: a voltage tester, a continuity tester, or a volt-ohm-milliammeter (VOM). With this equipment you'll be able to tell whether the electrical current is reaching and flowing through the part of the appliance you suspect is malfunctioning.

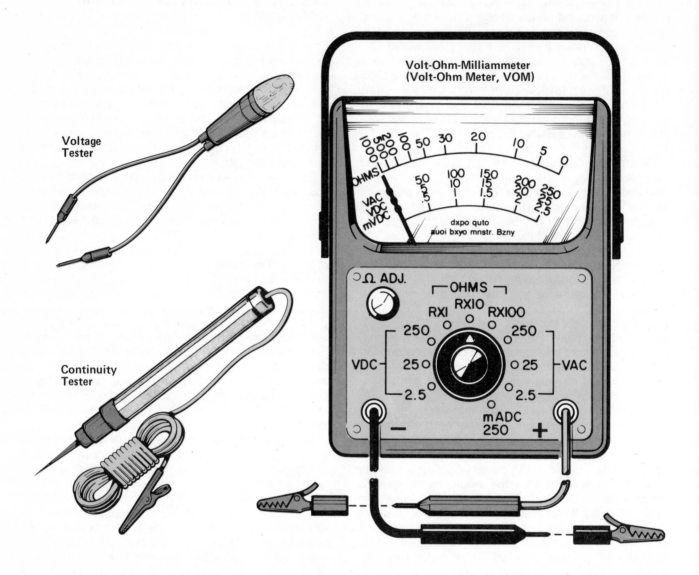

Volt-Ohm-Milliammeter
(Volt-Ohm Meter, VOM)

Voltage
Tester

Continuity
Tester

Testing devices you will need include a voltage tester (top left), a continuity tester (bottom left), and a volt-ohm-milliammeter or volt-ohm meter (VOM) (right).

Voltage Tester. The voltage tester is the simplest of these three tools. It consists of a small neon bulb with two insulated wires attached to the bottom of the bulb housing; each wire ends in a metal test probe. The voltage tester is used with the current turned on, to determine whether there is current flowing through a wire and to test for proper grounding. It is also sometimes used to determine whether adequate voltage is present. Look for a tester rated for up to 500 volts.

To use a voltage tester, touch one probe to one wire or connection and the other probe to the opposite wire or connection. If the component is receiving electricity, the light in the housing will glow; if the light doesn't glow, the trouble is at this point. For example, if you suspect that an electrical outlet is faulty, insert one probe of the tester into one slot in the outlet, and the other probe into the other slot. The light in the tester should light; if it doesn't, the outlet may be bad. To further test the outlet, pull it out of the wall. Place one probe of the tester on one terminal screw connection and the other probe on the other terminal screw. If the tester bulb lights, you know the outlet is malfunctioning —there is current flowing to the outlet, but it isn't flowing *through* the outlet to provide power to the appliance plugged into it. If the test bulb doesn't light, there is no current coming into the outlet. The problem may be a blown fuse or tripped circuit breaker, or the wire may be disconnected or broken behind the outlet.

Continuity Tester. The continuity tester, the primary diagnosis tool for many appliance repairs, consists of a battery in a housing, with a test probe connected to one end of the battery housing and a test wire with an alligator clip connected to the other end. The continuity tester is used with the current turned off, to determine whether a particular electrical component is carrying electricity and to pinpoint the cause of a malfunction.

To use a continuity tester, unplug the appliance and disassemble it to get at the component to be tested. *Caution: Do not use a continuity tester unless the appliance is unplugged or the power to the circuit is turned off.* Fasten the clip of the tester to one wire or connection of the component and touch the probe to the other wire or connection. If the component is receiving electricity and transmitting it, the tester will light or buzz; the circuit is continuous. If the tester doesn't light or buzz, or if it reacts only slightly, the component is faulty.

Volt-Ohm Meter (VOM). The voltage tester and the continuity tester are adequate for many diagnostic jobs, and they're fairly inexpensive. But for serious appliance troubleshooting and repairs, you should invest in a volt-ohm-milliammeter or volt-ohm meter (VOM), also known as a multitester. VOMs range in price from $10 to more than $100; you can buy one that's adequate for appliance testing for about $35. The VOM is battery-powered and is used with the current turned off. It's used to check continuity in a wire or component and to measure the electrical current—from 0 to 250 volts, AC or DC — flowing through the wire or component. *Caution: Do not use a VOM unless the appliance is unplugged or the power to the circuit is turned off.* The VOM is used with plug-in test leads, which may have probes at both ends or a probe at one end and an alligator clip at the other. An adjustment knob or switch is set to measure current on the scale desired, usually ohms; the dial indicates the current flowing through the component being tested.

The VOM is particularly useful for appliance testing because it is used while the power is turned off; there's no danger of electric shock while you're using it. It provides more precise information, in many cases, than the continuity tester, and so is preferable for testing many components. Learning to read a VOM is very easy, and manufacturers provide complete operating instructions with the meters. You can also buy information sheets on test readings of various electrical components used in appliances and in other applications, such as lights, switches, and outlets. Where a standard reading is available, this information has been included in the appliance repairs covered here. All readings are given in ohms; make sure you read the VOM dial on the ohms scale.

BASIC COMPONENTS

Regardless of how complex they are, appliances are put together with the same basic electrical components —electrical conductors, a cord and a plug, and various switches, sensors, and elements. All of these components can malfunction, and what looks like a total breakdown in an appliance is often traceable to the failure of a very simple component. For this reason, it's important to know how these basic electrical components work, why they fail, and how to repair or replace them. With this information, you can take care of many appliance problems very simply, with the minimum of effort and inconvenience.

Power Cords and Plugs

Many appliance "breakdowns" are really due to worn, frayed power cords or plugs that no longer make good electrical contact. To ensure safe operation, you should check all appliance cords for problems periodically, and replace frayed or broken cords immediately. When you suspect a cord is faulty, remove it from the appliance and test it with a continuity tester. Clip the tester to one blade of the plug, and touch the probe to one of the two wires—or, if it's a plug-in cord, insert the probe into one of the two holes—at the appliance end of the cord. If the tester lights or buzzes, move it to the other wire or hole and test again. Repeat this procedure to test the other blade of the plug. If the tester lights or buzzes at every test point, the cord is not faulty; if it fails to light or buzz at any point, the cord or the plug is faulty. You can pinpoint the defect by cutting off the plug and testing the cut end of the cord; if the tester lights or buzzes at all test points now, the plug is the defective part. The damaged component — cord or plug, or both—should be replaced.

Replacing a Cord. Replacing the cords on appliances, power tools, and other equipment is generally a simple chore. Some special cords can, and should, be bought as complete sets, with a plug attached to one end and special connection terminals attached to the other end. General-purpose cords can be fashioned from a separate plug, a length of an appropriate type of cord, and perhaps connection terminals as well. Electric ranges and clothes irons, for example, use complete-set-type cords; table saws and mixers use general-purpose cords. Always make sure you replace the old cord with a new one of the same type.

Often, the hardest part of the job is trying to determine how the appliance comes apart so that you can remove the old cord and attach a new one. Sometimes all you have to do is remove the cover from a connection box, as on a water pump. In other cases, as with a small hair dryer, the unit itself must be partially disassembled before you can reach the terminals. In nearly all cases, the cord is held in place by a clamp or by a

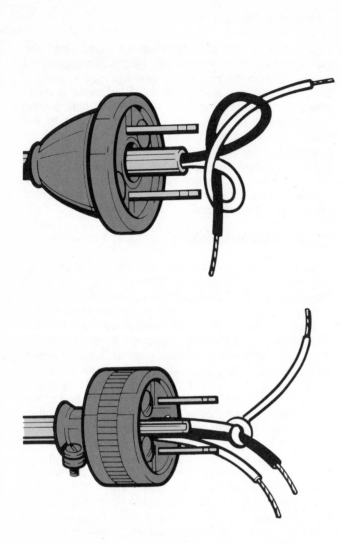

On a two-wire plug, tie a tight underwriters' knot with the inner wires (top). If there is a grounding wire, tie the knot as shown (bottom).

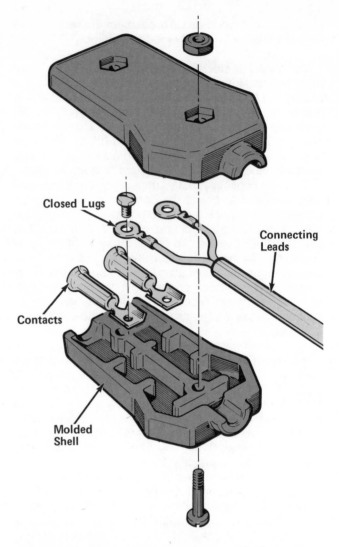

Closed Lugs

Connecting Leads

Contacts

Molded Shell

When a female plug malfunctions, open it and check the conductor wires. If the wires are loose, tighten the terminal screws. For other problems, replace the plug.

fitted strain-relief device. To remove the cord, unscrew the terminal screws or pull the pressure connectors apart, loosen the clamp or remove the strain-relief device, and pull the cord out. Installation of the new cord is simply a reverse procedure. Be sure to save the strain-relief device and replace it on the new cord. If you have to destroy the strain-relief device to remove it, replace it with a new one of the same type.

In some equipment, the conductor ends are looped around terminal screws, and making new connections is easy. Carefully strip off the outer insulation—not the insulation on the inner wires—for about three inches at the end of the cord. Then, with a wire stripper, remove about ½ inch of insulation from the end of each conductor wire. Twist the exposed filaments of each wire, clockwise, into a solid prong. Loosen the terminal

screws and loop each bare wire end clockwise around a screw; then tighten the screws firmly. Connect the wires at the appliance end of the new cord the same way the old ones were connected.

In some appliances, solderless connection terminals may be clamped to the old cord, and you'll have to fit replacement terminals to the new cord. This requires terminals of a matching kind, and a tool called a staker or crimper. You can find this tool at automotive or electrical supply stores. In a few cases, the terminals may be soldered to the conductor ends. You can replace them with solderless connection terminals.

Replacing a Plug. If only the plug of an appliance is faulty, you can attach a new plug to the old cord. Male plugs, with two blades or with two blades and a grounding prong, plug into an outlet. Female plugs, often used at the appliance end of the cord, have terminal holes instead of blades. Male plugs can usually be taken apart so you can get at the terminal screws. Female plugs may be held together by rivets or by screws; screw-held plugs can be taken apart, but rivet-held plugs cannot be repaired. When a plug malfunctions, open the plug, if possible, and check to make sure the conductor wires are properly attached to the plug's screw terminals. If the wires are loose, tighten the screw terminals. This may solve the problem; otherwise, the plug should be replaced.

To attach a new male plug, insert the cord end through the plug opening, and pull it through for about five or six inches. Carefully strip off the outer insulation —not the insulation on the inner wires—for about three inches, and then, with a wire stripper, remove about ½ inch of insulation from the end of each conductor wire. Twist the exposed filaments of each wire, clockwise, into a solid prong. After twisting the conductor ends, tie a tight underwriters' knot with the inner wires of the cord—follow the diagrams here to tie the knot. Then pull the plug down over the knot, leaving the exposed ends of the conductor wires sticking out. Loosen the terminal screws in the plug.

On a two-wire plug, loop each wire around one prong and toward a screw terminal. Loop the bare wire end clockwise around the screw terminal, and tighten the screw. If the screws are different colors (metals), connect the white wire to the white screw and the black wire to the yellow screw. On a three-wire plug, use the same technique to connect each of the three wires to a terminal screw. Connect the green grounding wire to the green screw terminal. When the conductor wires are firmly secured to the terminal screws, slide the cardboard insulator over the blades of the plug. If the plug has a clamp-type sleeve, clamp it firmly around the cord.

Gaskets

All appliances that use water or cold to do a job—and some that use heat—have gaskets, most commonly on the door. Gaskets do two things: they prevent leaks of water and air, and they increase the efficiency of the appliance. When a gasket fails, it should be replaced as soon as possible. To determine whether a gasket is faulty, inspect it for cracks and tears. It should feel spongy; if the gasket has hardened, it should be replaced. Replace a faulty gasket with a new one made specifically for the appliance; do not use a universal, fit-all gasket.

There are two basic types of gaskets, flush-mounted and channel-mounted. A flush-mounted gasket is secured to the door by a series of screws or clips, or held in place by a retaining strip or a panel. A channel-mounted gasket is held in a retaining groove; a special splining or gasket tool makes installation easier. Use

gasket cement to install either type of gasket, as recommended by the manufacturer.

First, remove the old gasket. If it's channel-mounted, pull it carefully out of the channel; if it's flush-mounted, remove the fasteners, retaining strip, or panel to release the gasket. Clean the gasket area thoroughly with warm water and liquid detergent, or, if necessary, with mineral spirits. Dry the door and then install the new gasket, smoothing it evenly into place and easing it around corners; use gasket cement if specified by the manufacturer. If you're installing a channel-mounted gasket, press it into place with a splining tool. Make sure the gasket is properly and smoothly positioned, with no part sticking up or curled under. Finally, replace the fasteners or the retaining strip or panel and its fasteners. Remove any excess gasket cement with mineral spirits; be careful not to damage the appliance's finish.

Wiring

Many appliance repair tasks involve wiring—connecting individual wires or groups of wires to install a new electrical component. The electrical wires in appliances may be connected in one of several ways, including the basic screw terminal connection, the push-in terminal, and sometimes the sleeve-type lug terminal. Wires may also be joined with the solderless connectors called wirenuts. Components that have many wires— washer timers, for instance, which control several operating cycles—are often connected in a wiring harness, a group of wires enclosed in a plastic sleeve. Each type of wire connection must be properly made when you install a new component, for each individual wire and each wire of a harness. Before you disconnect any wiring in an appliance, make sure you know how it's attached; when you install the new component, attach its wires the same way.

Switches

Switches operate by making contact with the conductor of an electrical circuit. When an appliance is plugged in, it's connected to a circuit in your home; power runs through the wires of the circuit to the appliance. When the appliance's on/off switch is turned on, the conductors of the appliance cord are moved into contact with the circuit conductors, and electricity flows through the switch to operate the appliance. The current flows in a loop through the appliance, making a complete circuit back through the switch to the line wires. Other basic appliance components are actually types or variations of switches — rheostats, thermostats, solenoids, and timers, for example, are all switches or secondary switches. These components operate inside appliances, to turn on motors, open and close valves, control heating elements, and turn on different parts of the appliance during different cycles, such as the rinse and

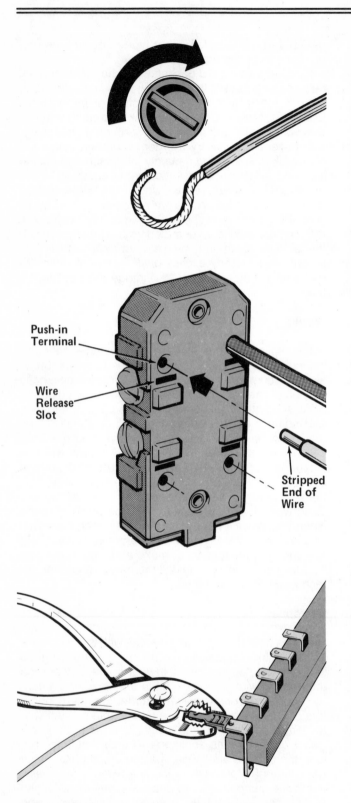

Push-in
Terminal

Wire
Release
Slot

Stripped
End of
Wire

The electrical wires in an appliance may be connected in one of several ways. In a screw terminal (top) each wire is looped around a screw; in a push-in terminal (center), the wire is simply plugged in. Sleeve-type lug terminals (bottom) use push-on connections, crimped into place.

spin cycles of a washer. There are several common types of switches — push buttons, toggles, rockers, slides, throw switches, and so on.

All switches are made up of electrical contacts in a mechanical housing, and switch failure can be caused by problems with either the contacts or the housing. When a switch malfunctions, turn it to the "on" position and watch to see if the contacts are moved into position so that they touch. If the contacts are not operating properly, the switch housing is faulty, and the switch should be replaced. If the switch's mechanical operation is all right, its contacts may be dirty or misaligned; if it has terminal screws, they may be loose. If the contacts are dirty or corroded, rub them gently with a fine emery board, and then with a soft cloth; if they're misaligned, bend them gently back into place. Tighten any loose terminal screws. If the contacts or screws are badly corroded, the switch should be replaced.

To determine whether a switch is working properly, disassemble the appliance to get at the switch, and test it with a continuity tester or a VOM, set to the R × 1 scale. With the appliance unplugged, hook the clip of the continuity tester to one lead of the switch and touch the probe to the other; or touch one probe of the VOM to each terminal. Turn the switch on. If the switch is functioning, the continuity tester will light or buzz, and will stop glowing or buzzing when the switch is turned off; or the VOM will read zero. If the tester doesn't light or buzz, or the VOM reads higher than zero, the switch is faulty, and should be replaced. Some switches should have a higher reading than zero, as detailed for each appliance. Use a new switch of the same type as the old one, and connect it exactly the same way.

Thermostats

A thermostat is a switch that controls temperature, in a heating element or a cooling device. Thermostats used in appliances may use a bimetallic strip, bimetallic thermodiscs, or a gas-filled bellows chamber to control the electrical contact. Faulty bimetallic-strip and thermodisc thermostats should be replaced. Gas-filled thermostats can sometimes be professionally repaired; where repair is feasible, it is much less expensive than replacement.

To determine whether a thermostat is functioning, disassemble the appliance to get at the thermostat, and test it with a continuity tester, or with a VOM set to the R × 1 scale. With the appliance unplugged, hook the clip of the continuity tester to one lead of the thermostat and touch the probe to the other; or touch one probe of the VOM to each terminal. The continuity tester should light or buzz; or the VOM should read zero. Turn down the temperature control dial; you'll see the contact points open at the thermostat. The tester should stop glowing or buzzing when the contacts open. If the thermostat is faulty, replace it with a new one of the same type.

Switch Control Devices

Many appliances perform several functions, such as the various cycles of a washer or dishwasher. These appliances operate automatically; once the on-off switch is turned on, switch components inside the appliance take over to control heat, water or fuel flow, motor speed, and other variables. The most important of these devices, used to operate switches, levers, and valves automatically, are solenoids, relays, and sensor/responder pairs.

Heating Elements

Heating elements work very simply. Unlike conductors, they are made of metal with high electrical resistance —usually a nickel-chrome alloy called nichrome. When current flows through the element, this high resistance prevents it from flowing easily; it must do work to get through the element, and this work is converted into heat. When the current is turned off, the element gradually cools. There are three types of heating elements: wire, ribbon, and rigid.

To determine whether a heating element is functioning, disassemble the appliance to get at the element, and test it with a continuity tester or a VOM, set to the R × 1 scale. With the appliance unplugged, hook the clip of the continuity tester to one terminal of the heating element and touch the probe to the other terminal; or hook one clip of the VOM to each terminal. If the element is functioning, the tester will light or buzz; or the VOM will read from 15 to 30 ohms. If the tester doesn't light or buzz, or the VOM reads higher than 30 ohms, the element is faulty, and should be replaced. If you use a continuity tester, however, look closely at the tester, especially if it's the light-up type—some heating elements have an extremely high resistance factor, and the light may produce only a dim glow or a faint buzz. This reaction does not mean that the element is faulty, but that it converts current to heat efficiently.

MAINTAINING AND REPAIRING APPLIANCE MOTORS

Depending on how much work it has to do, an appliance may be powered by one of several types of motors. Small appliances are usually powered by a universal motor, or, where less power is needed, by a shaded-pole or a synchronous motor. Larger appliances are usually powered by a split-phase or a ca-

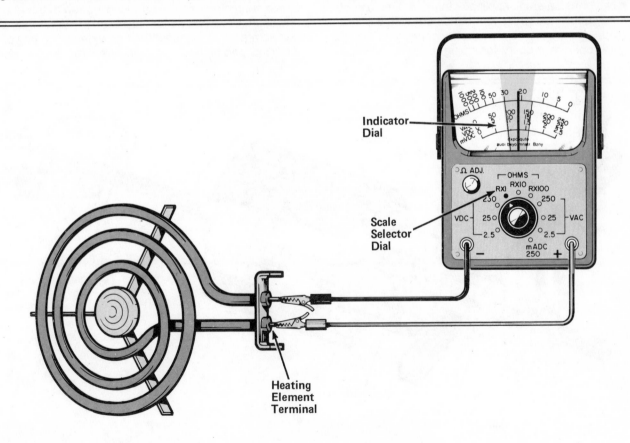

To test a heating element, use a VOM, set to the R x 1 scale, hook one tester clip to each of the element's terminals. The VOM should read from 15 to 30 ohms.

pacitor motor. Direct-current motors are used for small appliances that use batteries as the power source. Universal and direct-current motors have two blocks of carbon, called brushes, that function as electrical contacts. The other motors do not have brushes; they are all types of induction motors, in which a solid rotor spins inside a stationary piece called a stator. Both brush motors and induction motors are powered by the electromagnetic force created when electrical current passes through them.

Whatever their size and horsepower, appliance motors are usually dependable and long-wearing. You can prolong their life and increase their efficiency by keeping them clean and well lubricated. Use motor-driven appliances sensibly—don't overload them, don't abuse them, and don't ignore problems until they become serious.

There are several basic rules for operating motor-driven appliances:

- Always connect an appliance to an adequate power source; a 220-240-volt appliance must be connected to a 220-240-volt outlet. If the outlet for a major appliance is not grounded, use a grounded adapter plug to ground the appliance.
- Never use a small appliance that's wet, or operate any appliance while your hands are wet. If a large appliance, such as a washer or dryer, gets wet, *do not* operate it or try to unplug it. Have the motor

examined by a professional before you use the appliance again.
- Never overload an appliance. Overloading causes inefficient operation and motor overheating, and can cause excessive wear. If a motor turns off because it's overloaded, reduce the load before restarting the appliance.

Regular maintenance can forestall many motor problems. To prevent overheating and jamming, vacuum the motor housing periodically to remove dirt and lint. Make sure ventilation to the motor is adequate. At least once a year, oil the motor—if it has oil ports—with No. 30 nondetergent motor oil (not all-purpose oil). Procedures for specific appliances are detailed below.

Universal Motors. These motors consist of a rotor called an armature, with coils of wire wound around it, and a rotating cylinder called a commutator, with alternating strips of conducting and nonconducting material. The armature and the commutator are both mounted on the motor shaft. On each side of the commutator, a carbon brush carries current from the circuit. When the carbon brushes press against the commutator, the armature is magnetized and rotates. Most universal motors also have a cooling fan at the end of the shaft. Universal motors are used in many small and medium-size appliances; they provide strong power at both low and high speeds. Universal motors can oper-

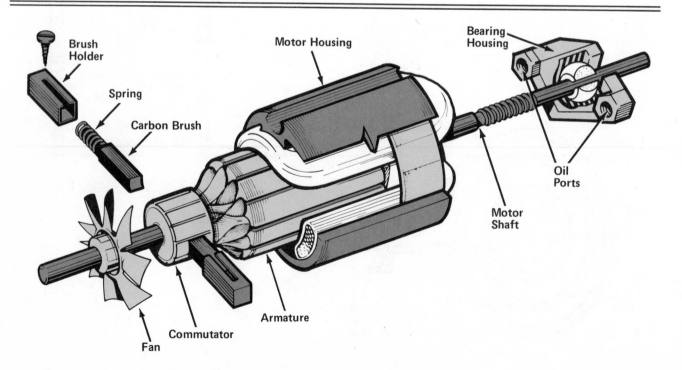

A universal motor has an armature and a rotating commutator, mounted on a motor shaft. Carbon brushes make the electrical contact; worn brushes are the most common problem.

ate on either AC or DC current. Their speed is controlled by a rheostat, a tapped-field control, a rectifier, or a governor, or by physical movement of the carbon brushes away from the armature.

Most universal motors are permanently lubricated and sealed by the manufacturer, and require no further attention. Some universal motors, however, have covered lubrication ports, usually marked "oil," at the ends of the motor shaft. This type of motor should be oiled every six months, or according to the manufacturer's instructions. Lift each port's lid and apply a drop or two of No. 30 nondetergent motor oil (not all-purpose oil).

Many universal motor malfunctions are caused by wearing down of the carbon brushes, the soft blocks of carbon that complete the electrical contact to the motor's commutator. When these brushes become worn, the motor will spark, and electrical contact may be incomplete. You can solve both problems by replacing the brushes.

Brushes can be checked visually or tested with a continuity tester. To sight-check them, remove the screws that hold the brushes and brush springs into the brush holders at the sides of the commutator. The screws will pop out of the screw holes; turn the motor over to tap out the brushes. The ends of the brushes should be curved to fit the commutator; if they're worn down short, new brushes are needed. To check carbon brushes with a continuity tester, remove the motor lead wires from the circuit. Tag the wires as you disconnect them so that you'll be able to reconnect them properly. Hook the tester clip to one motor lead and touch the probe to the other lead; the tester should light or buzz. Slowly revolve the motor shaft, keeping the tester in position. If the tester doesn't light or buzz, or if it flickers or stutters when you turn the motor shaft, the brushes should be replaced. If the springs behind the brushes are damaged, they should be replaced too.

Replace worn carbon brushes and damaged springs with new ones made specifically for the motor; the model information (number and make) is stamped on a metal plate fastened to the motor, or embossed on the metal housing of the motor. If you can't find the model information, take the worn brushes and springs with you to an appliance parts store to make sure you get the right kind. Insert the new springs and brushes in the brush holders, replace the brush assemblies, and secure the new brushes with the mounting screws that held the old brushes.

No other repairs should be attempted to a universal motor; if a serious malfunction occurs, buy a new motor or take the faulty motor to a professional for repairs. Most large universal motors are fastened to plate-type mountings; to remove the motor, disconnect the wires and remove the holding bolts and any belts that are present. If the faulty motor is in a small appliance, take the entire appliance to the repair shop. It may, however, be less expensive to buy a new appliance than to have the old one repaired.

Shaded-Pole Motors. These simple induction motors consist of a rotor cylinder turning inside an iron stator, with a wire coil on one side of the stator. Current flows through this coil to create a magnetic field in the stator and start the rotor turning. Shaded-pole motors provide very little power; they are used in small appliances such as small fans. They operate on AC current. Shaded-pole motors that operate at a precise, consistent speed are called synchronous motors; they're used in clocks, timers, and similar appliances where accuracy is important and strong power is not necessary.

Shaded-pole and synchronous motors require no maintenance except cleaning, as detailed above. Most malfunctions are caused by a faulty starter coil, and can be corrected by replacement of the coil with a new one of the same make and model number. To replace the coil, unscrew the frame of the motor and open the halves of the frame. Disconnect the old coil and remove it. Finally, insert the new coil and connect it the same way the old coil was connected. If the motor frame is riveted together—and many are—the coil is not worth the work of replacement; instead, replace the appliance.

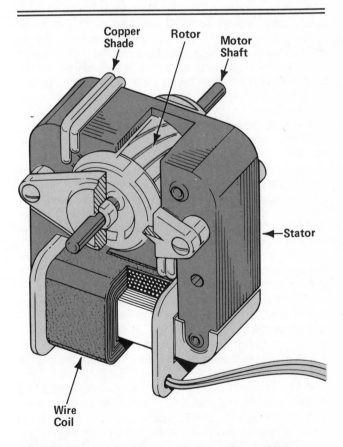

A shaded-pole motor consists of a rotor turning inside a stator on the motor shaft, with a wire coil on one side of the stator.

Large Appliances

Because major appliances constitute a major investment, their maintenance and repair is very important. Most appliances of the same type operate on the same basic principles, so repairs to most models are similar or identical, no matter what brand or make is involved. Although different makes of appliances generally operate alike, however, they don't conform to the same design; major brand-name appliances may look quite different. To make it even more complicated, manufacturers, in order to beat their competition, build their appliances with all sorts of extra features. Many of these extras are real value-added innovations; others, unfortunately, are not. Because of the differences among brand-name appliances, you should use the repair and replacement techniques in this chapter as general guidelines, not as absolute standards for specific models.

Because appliance operation does follow the same principles, it's easy to be tempted into buying repair parts that look alike or "fit all." This is not a good idea—replacement parts *must* match the make and model of the appliance being repaired. Most appliances have a metal tag, attached to the back service panel, that provides the model, make, and other identification information. If the tag is missing, look for this information embossed or stamped onto a service panel. If you can't find this information, take the malfunctioning part to an appliance parts store or an appliance repair shop that sells replacement parts. The dealer should be able to identify the part for you and provide the proper replacement. If the appliance is riveted or welded together, don't try to disassemble it; you could do more harm than good. Call a professional service person, or, if possible, take the entire appliance in to a professional service center.

While you will be able to handle many parts *replacement* jobs yourself, you probably won't be able to handle many parts *repair* jobs — you probably don't have the skill or own the specialized equipment necessary for them, and it isn't recommended that you invest in such specialized equipment. Moreover, it's often less expensive to replace a part than to repair it. If you aren't sure replacement is worth it, call a repair shop for an estimate. You can save the expense of a service call, though, by removing the malfunctioning part yourself and taking it in to be tested and/or repaired. In the same way, you can save the cost of installation by installing the new part yourself.

Air Conditioners

Air conditioners consist, very simply, of a refrigerant in two coils, a condenser and an evaporator. At the condenser, a compressor pressurizes the refrigerant, lowering its temperature. The pressurized coolant flows from the condenser coil to the evaporator coil, where air is cooled by contact with the coil and the coolant picks up heat from the air. Then the warmed coolant flows back to the condenser to be repressurized.

In central air-conditioning systems, the condenser and the evaporator are separate, but in room air conditioners, all of the appliance's components are contained in one housing. The condenser coil faces outside; the evaporator faces inside. Sandwiched between the coils are a compressor, fan, a motor, and the thermostat control. The coils, the compressor, and the motor of a room air conditioner are sealed components, so any repairs to them should be left to a professional service person. You can make minor repairs, though, and regular maintenance will keep your unit running well. When extensive repairs are needed, you can also save the cost of a service call by removing the air conditioner from its mounting and taking it to the repair shop.

During the winter, room air conditioners should be protected from the elements; either remove the unit from its mounting and store it, or cover the outside portion of the unit with a commercial room air conditioner cover or with heavy plastic sheeting, held with duct tape. Air conditioner covers are available at hardware stores, home centers, and appliance outlets.

Caution: Before doing any work on an air conditioner, make sure it's unplugged. Room air conditioners have one or two capacitors, located behind the control panel and near the fan. Capacitors store electricity, even when the power to the unit is turned off. Before you do any work on an air conditioner, you must unplug it and discharge the capacitor, or you could receive a severe shock.

First, unplug the air conditioner or turn off the power to the circuit. To gain access to the capacitor—there may be one or two—remove the unit's control panel. The capacitor is located behind the control panel and near the fan; it looks like a large dry-cell battery. To discharge the capacitor, use a 20,000-ohm, 2-watt resistor, an inexpensive wire unit available at most elec-

trical supply stores. Fasten the clips of the resistor to the terminals of the capacitor; this discharges the capacitor. If the capacitor has three terminal posts, connect the resistor to one outer terminal and the center terminal; then to the other outside terminal and the center terminal. After discharging the capacitor, you can proceed to make the necessary repairs.

Filter. At the beginning of every cooling season, and once a month during the season, remove the front grille and clean or replace the filter. If you live in a very dusty area, clean or replace the filter more often. Most room air conditioners have a washable filter, which looks like sponge rubber. Clean the filter with a solution of mild household detergent and water; rinse well. Let the filter dry completely before reinstalling it. Some units have a throw-away filter, similar to a furnace filter. When this type of filter becomes dirty, replace it with a new one of the same type.

Evaporator and Condenser Coils. Clean the evaporator and condenser coils at the beginning of the

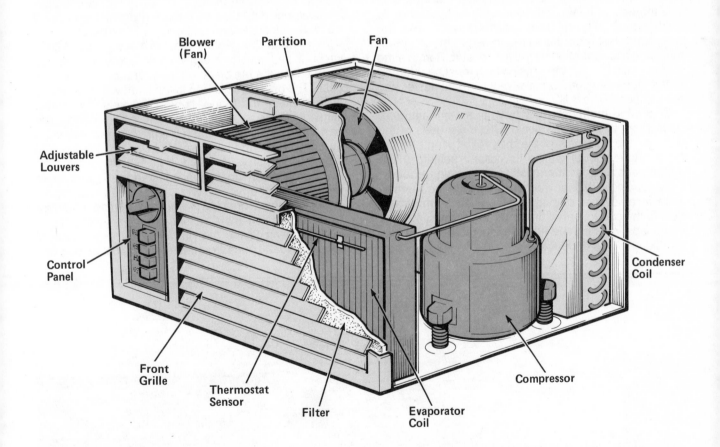

Both of the major components of a room air conditioner are contained in one housing. The condenser coil faces outside; the evaporator coil faces inside.

cooling season and every month during the season; if you live in a very dusty area, clean the coils more often. Use a vacuum cleaner on these components. If the fins on the coils are bent, straighten them with a fin comb, sold at most appliance parts outlets. Fin combs are designed to slide into the spaces between the fins. Use the fin comb carefully; the fins are made of light-gauge aluminum, and are easily damaged.

Switch. The selector switch, directly behind the control panel, turns the unit on. If the air conditioner does not run at any setting, and it is receiving power, chances are the switch is faulty. To correct the problem, remove the control panel and locate the switch. Check the switch terminals for burnt insulation or burn-like marks on the terminals; if you see any indication of burning, replace the switch with a new one of the same type. The switch is held to the control panel or frame with screws; unscrew it and connect the new one the same way. If you determine that the problem may not be the switch, call a professional service person.

Thermostat. The thermostat is located behind the control panel; to test and/or replace this component, remove the grille and the control panel from the unit. The thermostat has a special sensing bulb attached to it; this part extends from the thermostat into the evaporator coil area. Its role is to sense the temperature, which is controlled by the thermostat. Remove the thermostat carefully; the sensing bulb must be returned to the identical spot. To make replacement easier, tag the location of the bulb.

Check the thermostat with a volt-ohm-milliammeter (VOM), set to the R × 1 scale. Clip the probes of the tester to the terminals of the thermostat, and turn the temperature control dial to its coldest setting. If the meter reads zero, the thermostat is functioning properly; if the reading is higher than zero, replace the thermostat with a new one of the same type. The thermostat is held to the control panel or frame with screws, clips, or metal tabs; connect the new thermostat the same way the old one was connected.

If the thermostat has more than two lead wires connected to it—not counting the sensing bulb wire—do not try to test or replace it; call a professional service person. For detailed instructions on using a VOM, see the chapter on appliances.

Drain Ports. As the air conditioner operates, condensed moisture and water vapor from the evaporator coil are funneled through drain ports or an opening between the partition or barrier between the evaporator coil and the condenser coil. At this point, the fan blows the moisture against the condenser coil, where the water is dissipated. These drain ports can become clogged with dirt. The result is water leaking from the appliance, usually through the bottom of the grille. To prevent clogging, clean the ports with a short piece of clothes hanger wire or the blade of a pocket knife, at the beginning of every cooling season and every month during the season. Also check the condenser side of the air conditioner. Some models have a drain port along the bottom edge of the cabinet frame. If your air conditioner has this drain port, clean it out when you clean the other ports.

Fan. When a fan malfunctions, the problem is usually loose or dirty blades. If the fan doesn't work, or if it's noisy, cleaning and tightening will usually fix it.

First, open the cabinet and locate the fan. With a vacuum and/or a soft cloth, clean away any debris. Then check the fan blade on the motor shaft for looseness. The blade is fastened to the shaft with a setscrew at the hub of the blade; tighten the setscrew with a screwdriver or an Allen wrench. If the air conditioner has a round vent fan, tighten the fan on the motor shaft by inserting a long-bladed screwdriver through a port in the fan. The fan is installed in its housing with bolts, and vibration can loosen these fasteners. Tighten them with a wrench.

Most air conditioner fan motors are permanently lubricated and sealed at the factory, but some have oil ports for lubrication. If the fan has oil ports, apply several drops of No. 20 nondetergent motor oil (not all-purpose

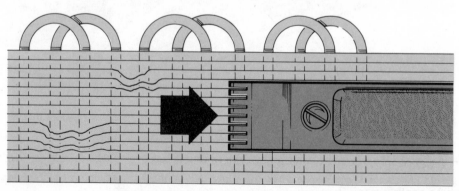

If the fins on the condenser coil are bent, straighten them with a fin comb. Use the comb carefully; the fins are made of light-gauge aluminum, and are easily damaged.

oil) to each port at the beginning of the cooling season.

If you suspect the fan motor is faulty, test it with a VOM. Disconnect the terminal wires from the terminals and clip the probes of the VOM, set to the R × 1 scale, to the wires. If the meter reads between about 3 and 30 ohms, the motor is functioning properly; if the meter reads either zero or extremely high, replace the motor. To remove the motor, remove the fan, the power wires, and several mounting bolts; install the new motor with the reverse procedure. If the condenser coil must be

Room Air Conditioner Troubleshooting Chart

Caution: Disconnect power before inspecting or repairing.

PROBLEM	POSSIBLE CAUSE	SOLUTION
Unit doesn't run	1. No power.	1. Check power cord, plug, and outlet. Check for blown fuses or tripped circuit breaker at main entrance panel; restore circuit.
	2. Motor overload or safety shutoff.	2. Wait 30 minutes; press reset button. Repeat if necessary.
	3. Switch faulty.	3. Check terminals and insulation; if burns are evident, replace switch. If switch looks all right, call a professional.
Fuses blow	1. Circuit overloaded.	1. Put on different circuit.
	2. Voltage low.	2. Call a professional or the power company.
Unit doesn't cool	1. Thermostat set too high.	1. Lower thermostat setting 5 degrees.
	2. Filter dirty.	2. Clean or replace filter.
	3. Coils dirty.	3. Clean coils.
	4. Condenser blocked from outside.	4. Make sure outside of unit is not blocked.
	5. Motor faulty.	5. Call a professional.
	6. Compressor faulty.	6. Call a professional.
	7. Coolant leak.	7. Call a professional.
Fan runs, but unit doesn't cool	1. Thermostat set too high.	1. Lower thermostat setting 5 degrees.
	2. Thermostat faulty.	2. Test thermostat; if faulty, replace or call a professional.
	3. Coils dirty.	3. Clean coils.
	4. Motor faulty.	4. Call a professional.
	5. Compressor faulty.	5. Call a professional.
Unit cools, but fan doesn't run	1. Control switch set wrong.	1. Reset switch; try different settings.
	2. Fan clogged.	2. Clean and tighten fan blades.
	3. Fan blades bent.	3. Straighten fan blades.
	4. Fan motor faulty.	4. Replace fan motor or call a professional.
Unit turns on and off repeatedly	1. Coils dirty.	1. Clean coils.
	2. Filter dirty.	2. Clean or replace filter.

moved to get the fan out, however, do not try to remove the motor; call a professional service person. For detailed instructions on using a VOM, see the chapter on appliances.

Motor and Compressor. If problems occur in the motor or compressor of the air conditioner, call a professional service person.

Dishwashers

The control panels on the latest dishwashers can look intimidating—they're loaded with so many dials, push buttons, lights, clocks, and other features that the machine looks too complex to repair. But this is actually not the case. With the exception of the control panel, dishwashers haven't changed much in basic design over the last 10 years. You can repair most dishwasher malfunctions, and the repair procedures are relatively simple.

Caution: Because the dishwasher is connected to both the plumbing system and the electrical system, you must consider both systems when working on this appliance. Before doing any work on the dishwasher, make sure the unit is unplugged or the power to the unit is turned off; remove the fuse or trip the circuit breaker that controls the circuit, at the main entrance panel or at a separate panel. Shut off the water supply to the dishwasher at the shutoff in the basement or crawl space under the kitchen.

Basic Operating Checks. If the dishwasher doesn't run, first check to make sure it's receiving power. If the unit plugs into a wall outlet, check the cord, the plug, and the outlet to make sure they're functioning properly. Most dishwashers are wired directly into a circuit; check the main entrance panel for a blown fuse or tripped circuit breaker, and restore the circuit. If your home is an older one, the dishwasher may be wired to a separate entrance panel; look for a blown fuse or breaker at this panel, and restore the circuit. If the circuit is receiving power, and the wall outlet is controlled by a switch, the switch may be faulty. Test the switch with a voltage tester. Take off the switch cover plate; place one probe of the tester on one terminal and the other probe on the other terminal. If the tester bulb lights, the switch is functioning; if it doesn't light, the switch is faulty. Replace the switch with a new one of the same type; connect the wires exactly the same way they were connected to the old switch. *Caution: Make sure the power to the circuit is turned off before you replace the switch.*

Second, make sure the door is tightly closed and latched; the dishwasher will not operate until the latch is properly engaged. To check the latch, close and latch the door, and hold the latch tightly in place. Then, still pressing the latch closed, turn the control knob to "on." If the dishwasher works, the latch is faulty, and should be replaced.

Third, make sure the water is turned on, and the water temperature is high enough. A breakdown in the water heater could stop the flow of water to the dishwasher. Try the hot water in the kitchen sink or lavatory. If you can draw hot water, the water heater may not be at fault. For best results, the water heater should be set no lower than 140° F.

Finally, make sure the controls on the control panel are properly set. The newer push-button controls can be very sensitive; make sure the buttons are *firmly* pressed into position.

Door Gasket. If water leaks through the dishwasher door, the gasket is probably faulty. Open the door and examine the gasket. It should be soft and resilient; if it's worn, cracked or hard, it should be replaced. To replace a gasket, buy a gasket made specifically for the model dishwasher you own. Install the new gasket as detailed in the section on gaskets in "Basic Appliance Repair Principles."

Door Latch. The latch on a dishwasher door is opened and closed repeatedly, and this hard use can lead to mechanical problems—the latch may be loose, or may have slipped out of position, throwing the alignment off and preventing the door from closing properly. When this happens, the latch does not engage properly, and the dishwasher will not start. In many cases, you may be able to solve the problem by adjusting the position of the latch. Move the latch slightly by loosening the screws that hold it, and slide the latch with your fingers or pliers. The screw slots are made especially for this purpose. Close and open the door to see where the latch is properly aligned, and tighten the screws to hold it in place in the correct position.

After repositioning the latch, check to see if it's working properly. Close and latch the door, and turn the control knob to "on." If the dishwasher doesn't start, the latch is faulty. Replace it with a new latch; connect it the same way the old one is connected. You may have to move the new latch back and forth several times before it works properly.

Door Switch. On many dishwashers, the latch engages a switch to activate the timer and other control components; if the latch is not completely engaged or the switch is faulty, the machine will not operate. To determine whether the switch is faulty, latch the door and hold the latch tightly in the closed position. This works best on a unit with a lever-type latch. Then turn

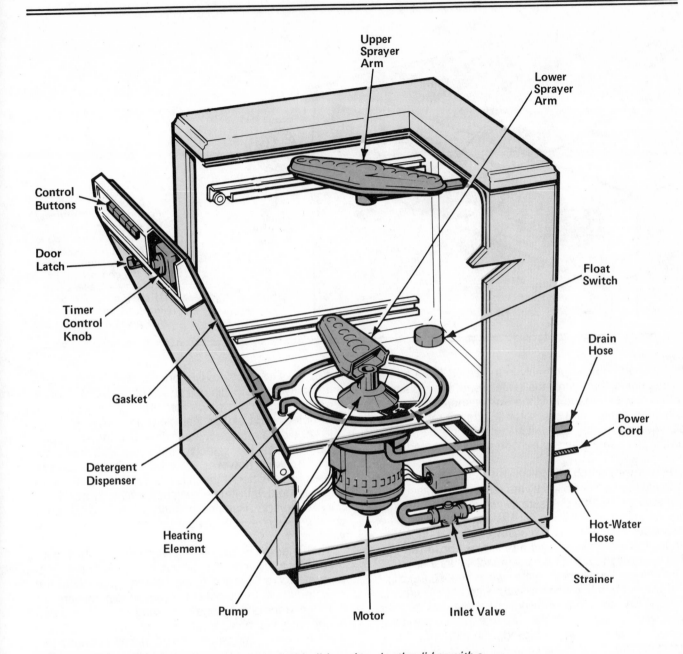

Upper Sprayer Arm

Lower Sprayer Arm

Control Buttons

Door Latch

Timer Control Knob

Gasket

Detergent Dispenser

Heating Element

Pump

Motor

Inlet Valve

Float Switch

Drain Hose

Power Cord

Hot-Water Hose

Strainer

Dishwashers spray hot water into a tub stacked with dishes, then dry the dishes with a blower or heating element. Problems often involve the water supply and drainage systems.

the control to the "on" position. If the unit works, the problem is probably a misaligned lock unit; adjust the lock unit with a screwdriver. If this doesn't solve the problem, the switch may be faulty.

Test the switch with a VOM, set to the R × 1 scale. Clip one probe of the VOM to each switch terminal, and shut the dishwasher's door. If the meter reads zero, the switch is working. If the meter reads higher than zero, the switch is faulty, and should be replaced. Replace the switch with a new one of the same type; connect the new switch the same way.

Float Switch. Dishwashers are usually protected from overfilling by a float switch. This switch is located in the bottom of the unit; to get at it, open the door and remove the bottom dish rack. If water overfilling is a problem, the float switch may be stuck. Clean away any food debris around the float. With a screwdriver handle, lightly tap the top of the float; this may free it.

If tapping doesn't work, remove the lower access panel and locate the bottom portion of the float and float switch. Test the float switch with a VOM, set to the R × 1 scale. If the meter reads zero, the switch is not

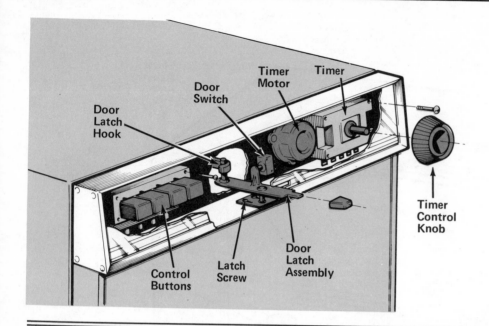

Door Latch Hook · Door Switch · Timer Motor · Timer · Timer Control Knob · Door Latch Assembly · Latch Screw · Control Buttons

For repairs to the timer, door latch, or switches, remove the control panel. To take it off, remove a series of retaining screws and the control knobs, and lift the panel off. If the timer is faulty, don't try to fix it; replace it with a new one.

faulty; the trouble is probably in the timer. If the meter reads higher than zero, the switch is faulty; replace it with a new one made to fit the dishwasher. The switch is held to a mounting bracket with screws; remove the screws to get the old switch out. Connect the new switch the same way the old one was connected.

Pressure Switch. Although the water level in most dishwashers is controlled by the timer, some machines are equipped with a pressure switch that does this job. You can quickly tell if your unit has one by removing the lower access panel. The pressure switch is mounted under the tub housing, and has a small hose running into it, about the size of a car windshield washer hose. The hose is usually held to the switch by a spring clip.

If the dishwasher won't fill with water, lightly tap the switch housing with a screwdriver handle; this may jar the switch loose. Also make sure that the hose and the spring clip are properly attached, and that the hose is not defective. Tighten the connections and replace the hose, if necessary. If this doesn't solve the problem, test the switch with a VOM, set to the R × 1 scale. If the meter reads zero, the switch is functioning; if it reads higher than zero, the switch is faulty, and should be replaced. Replace the switch with a new one made for the dishwasher. The switch is held to the tub with retaining screws; remove the screws to take out the old switch. Connect the new switch the same way the old one was connected.

Timer and Control Switches. The timer controls many operations, and a faulty timer can cause many problems. Because the timer is a complex component, don't try to fix it; if it's faulty, replace it with a new timer made for the dishwasher. Test the timer with a VOM,

set to the R × 1 scale. Disconnect one of the timer's terminal wires, and clip one probe of the VOM to each terminal. If the meter reads zero, the timer is working; if the meter reads higher than zero, the timer is faulty, and should be replaced. If possible, use the same procedure to test the selector and cycle switches. The wiring hookup, however, may be too complicated to figure out on either of these switches. If you aren't sure you can deal with these switches, call a professional service person. Replace a faulty timer — or a faulty control switch — with a new one made for the dishwasher.

The timer is connected to several wires, which supply power to operate the various functions of the dishwasher. To replace the timer, have a helper hold the new timer next to the old one, and connect the wires of the new timer one by one, removing the old wire and connecting the new, to make sure you connect the wires correctly. The wires may be friction-fit on the terminals; if they are, use long-nosed pliers to remove the wires. Don't pull up on the wires or you may break the connection between the wires and the clips. After connecting the wires, set the new timer in position, secure it the way the old one was secured, and replace the control panel and knobs.

Water Inlet Valve. The water inlet valve controls the amount of water flowing into the dishwasher; it may be activated by the timer or by a solenoid. If the dishwasher doesn't fill with water, first make sure that the water supply to the unit is turned on, and that there's no problem at the water heater—a shutdown of the water heater would cause a shutdown of the water to the dishwasher. Finally, check the timer to make sure it's working through its programmed sequences. If both the water supply and the timer are in working order, the problem is probably in the inlet valve.

The inlet valve is located under the tub of the dishwasher. If the valve is controlled by a solenoid, the solenoid is usually connected to the side of the unit. Tap the solenoid and the valve lightly with the handle of a screwdriver; then start the dishwasher again. If the dishwasher still doesn't fill, test the solenoid with a VOM, set to the R × 1 scale. If the meter reads from about 100 to 1,000, the solenoid is functioning. If the reading is higher than 1,000, the solenoid is faulty, and should be replaced. Replace the solenoid with a new one of the same size and type; connect the new solenoid the same way the old one was connected.

Malfunctions of the inlet valve may also occur when a screen inside the valve becomes clogged with mineral deposits. To solve this problem, pry out the screen with a screwdriver and flush it thoroughly with running water; then replace it in the valve.

Badly worn or misshapen inlet valves cannot be repaired; if the valve is damaged, replace it with a new one made for the dishwasher. The valve is usually held to a mounting bracket with screws. Take apart the connection linking the valve to the water supply; then take out the screws and remove the valve. Install the new valve by making the connections in reverse order.

Drain Valves. Some dishwashers have drain valves; these valves are used only in dishwashers with non-reversible motors. If you can't tell from the manufacturer's operating instructions whether your dishwasher has a drain valve, or a nonreversible motor, remove the bottom panel of the unit and locate the motor. If the motor has two or three wires running into it, the motor is nonreversible. When the drain valve malfunctions, follow the procedures detailed below for water pumps; if this doesn't solve the problem, call a professional service person.

Heating Element. This component is used to help dry the dishes. In most dishwashers, the heating element fits around the screen in the bottom of the tub housing; it looks like a round version of an electric oven element. The heating element doesn't malfunction often, but it can burn out. If you suspect a faulty element, test it with a VOM, set to the R × 1 scale. If the meter reads between 15 and 30 ohms, the element is working; if the reading is higher than 30 ohms, the element is faulty, and should be replaced. Replace it with a new one made for the dishwasher. Disconnect the electrical leads to the element's terminal screws, and remove the nuts or other fasteners that hold the element to the terminals. From inside the tub, lift the element out. It may be held by clips and ceramic blocks in the tub, but you can easily thread it past these spacers. Set the new heating element in position, reconnect the power leads, and replace the fasteners that hold the element in place.

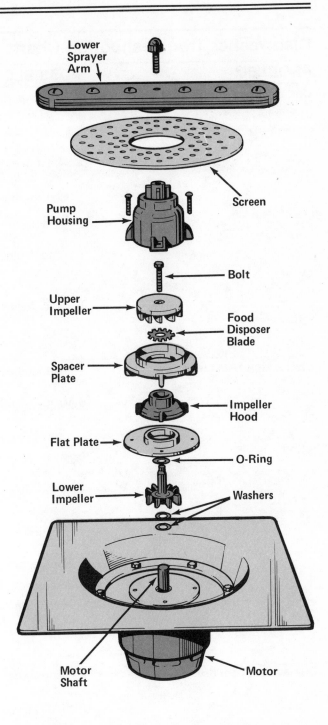

To reach the water pump, remove the sprayer arm and screen and then the pump housing. Remove a bolt, and the pump components can be disassembled.

Blower. Some dishwashers use a blower unit instead of a heating element to dry the dishes. The blower forces hot air through the dishwasher tub; it is located under the tub, not in it. If the blower system malfunctions, don't try to fix it yourself; call a profes-

23

Dishwasher Troubleshooting Chart

PROBLEM	POSSIBLE CAUSE	SOLUTION
Unit doesn't run	1. No power.	1. Check power cord, plug, and outlet. Check for blown fuses or tripped circuit breakers at main entrance panel; restore circuit.
	2. Motor overloaded or safety shutoff faulty.	2. Press reset button on control panel.
	3. Controls not properly set.	3. Set controls properly.
	4. Door not latched.	4. Close door so latch engages; if latch faulty, replace.
	5. Timer faulty.	5. Make sure timer is properly set. Test timer; if faulty, replace.
	6. Motor faulty.	6. Check motor leads for proper connections. Remove motor and take to a professional, or replace motor.
Dishes don't get clean	1. Inadequate preparation.	1. Scrape and rinse dishes before loading machine.
	2. Water not hot enough.	2. Set water heater thermostat at 140° to 150° F.
	3. Soap dispenser blocked, clogged, or broken.	3. Leave dispenser exposed when loading machine. Clean dispenser; if broken, replace.
	4. Wrong type of detergent.	4. Use detergent recommended for dishwashers.
	5. Detergent ineffective or spoiled.	5. Use new detergent.
	6. Sprayer arm clogged.	6. Clean sprayer arm.
	7. Strainer clogged.	7. Clean strainer.
	8. Pump clogged.	8. Clean pump.
	9. Timer faulty.	9. Make sure timer is properly set. Test timer; if faulty, replace.
Dishes don't get dry	1. Dishes removed too soon after end of cycle.	1. Wait until hot water has had time to evaporate from dishes.
	2. Poor stacking.	2. Stack dishes so there is air space around them.
	3. Water not hot enough.	3. Set water heater thermostat to 140° to 150° F.
	4. Heating element faulty.	4. Test element; if faulty, replace.
	5. Wetting agent gone.	5. Check dispenser; if necessary, refill.
	6. Leaky water inlet valve.	6. Clean water inlet valve; if damaged, replace valve.

Dishwasher Troubleshooting Chart (Continued)

PROBLEM	POSSIBLE CAUSE	SOLUTION
Dishes don't get dry (continued)	7. Fan motor faulty.	7. Clean fan assembly; check fan terminals for proper connections. If necessary, replace fan.
Dishwasher doesn't fill	1. Float switch stuck.	1. Clean float and float switch; tap lightly with screwdriver handle. If necessary, replace float switch.
	2. Timer faulty.	2. Make sure timer is properly set. Test timer; if faulty, replace.
	3. Water inlet valve screens clogged.	3. Clean water inlet valve screens.
	4. Water inlet valve solenoids faulty.	4. Tap solenoids lightly with screwdriver handle; if no result, replace water inlet valves.
	5. Drain valve stuck open.	5. Call a professional.
	6. Pressure switch faulty.	6. Replace switch.
	7. Water not turned on.	7. Check valve under dishwasher. Open hot water faucet in kitchen sink; if water doesn't flow, check for problems at water heater.
	8. Water pressure low.	8. Call water company.
Water doesn't drain	1. Impeller jammed.	1. Clean impeller; if faulty, replace.
	2. Drain valve solenoid faulty.	2. Tap solenoid lightly with screwdriver handle; if no result, call a professional.
	3. Drain valve clogged.	3. Clean drain valve.
	4. Drain hose kinked.	4. Straighten drain hose.
	5. Strainer clogged.	5. Clean strainer.
	6. Pump faulty.	6. Clean pump; if no result, replace pump.
	7. Motor faulty.	7. Call a professional.
Dishwasher doesn't shut off	1. Timer faulty.	1. Make sure timer is properly set. Test timer; if faulty, replace.
	2. Float switch stuck.	2. Clean float switch; tap switch lightly with screwdriver handle. If no result, replace float switch.
	3. Water inlet valve clogged or stuck open.	3. Disassemble and clean water inlet valve.

Dishwasher Troubleshooting Chart (Continued)

PROBLEM	POSSIBLE CAUSE	SOLUTION
Dishwasher runs while door is open	1. Door switch faulty.	1. Replace door switch.
	2. Motor faulty.	2. Call a professional, or remove motor and take to a professional.
Water leaks	1. Poor stacking.	1. Stack dishes so there is air space around them.
	2. Too much detergent.	2. Use amount of detergent recommended by manufacturer.
	3. Door gasket worn or damaged.	3. Replace gasket.
	4. Timer faulty.	4. Make sure timer is properly set. Test timer; if faulty, replace.
	5. Water inlet valve stuck open.	5. Clean water inlet valve; if damaged, replace.
	6. Pump seal faulty.	6. Call a professional.
	7. Hose loose or damaged.	7. Tighten hose connections; if hose damaged, replace.
	8. Door hinges broken or misaligned.	8. Tighten and realign hinges; if necessary, replace hinges.
Noisy operation	1. Poor stacking.	1. Make sure dishes are properly stacked.
	2. Machine out of level.	2. Level unit with shims; check level from front to back and side to side.
	3. Sprayer arms misaligned.	3. Adjust sprayer arms so they don't scrape against screens or racks.
	4. Water level low.	4. Refrain from using washer, shower, and toilets while dishwasher is operating.
Racks stick	1. Door not open.	1. Make sure door is fully open when racks are pulled out.
	2. Racks off tracks.	2. Guide racks into tracks.
	3. Rack guides and glides dirty or misaligned.	3. Adjust and clean rack bearing points.
	4. Rack guides damaged.	4. Replace rack guides.

sional repair person. Before you call for service, though, make sure that the power is on and the timer is working.

Sprayer Arms. The sprayer arms seldom cause any trouble, but sometimes the spray holes in the arms become crusted with detergent. When this happens, the holes must be cleaned out so that the arms will work efficiently. Remove the lower arm by twisting off the cap that holds it to the motor shaft; wash it thoroughly with water and mild household detergent. Sharpen a lead pencil and break off the lead point;

use the tapered end of the pencil to ream out the holes. A wood manicure stick can also be used. Do *not* use toothpicks, matches, or metal objects for this job—lightweight wooden sticks could break off in the ports, causing blockage; metal could scrape and enlarge the ports. After cleaning, place the sprayer arm back on the motor shaft, and twist the cap back on to hold it in place. Follow the same procedure to clean the upper sprayer arm.

Strainer. The strainer is located directly under the lower sprayer arm. When the strainer becomes clogged with food and detergent debris, the dishwasher may flood or overfill. On some dishwashers, the strainer is a plastic or metal component consisting of two semicircular halves; to remove this type of strainer, pry it up. On other dishwashers, the strainer is a one-piece component; to remove this type, remove the cap that holds the sprayer arm on its shaft, and then remove the sprayer arm and the strainer.

Wash the strainer in the kitchen sink, with water and mild household detergent. Use a fairly stiff brush to get the debris out of the holes and slots in the strainer. Rinse the strainer well and replace it. If part of the strainer lifts out for regular cleaning, check it and clean it, if necessary, after each load of dishes is washed.

Leaks. If the dishwasher leaks and you know the problem is not related to tub overfilling, the pump, or inlet valve problems, the plumbing connections may be faulty. Most dishwashers are connected to the water supply with metal pipe and fittings; the leak could be at these fittings. If the fittings are threaded—not soldered — tighten them with an adjustable wrench. If this doesn't work, chances are the threads are stripped, or the fitting is cracked or otherwise damaged. In this case, replace the fitting with a new one of the same type. You may need additional information on making pipe repairs; if necessary, consult a book on plumbing.

Most dishwashers discharge used water through a pipe or a hose connected to the garbage disposer under the kitchen sink. If the drain line is flexible hosing, it may have cracked from prolonged exposure to hot water. Examine the hose and, if it's damaged, replace it. If the hose is leaking at its connections with the disposer or dishwasher, tighten the fittings or clamps at the connections, or replace the clamps. Also check for water leaks around inlet valves, drain valves, and wherever you see flexible hoses and hose connections. Leaks at clamps can be stopped by tightening or replacing the clamps; leaks in hoses can be eliminated by replacing the hoses.

Water Pump. In most dishwashers, the water pump is located under the lower sprayer arm. This component pumps the water through the dishwasher. The pump has two impellers—top and bottom—and these, as well as other components, can become clogged with food or detergent. To disassemble the pump, remove the cap that holds the sprayer arm on. Then, in sequence, take off the sprayer arm, the screen, the pump housing, a bolt, the upper impeller, the food disposer blade, a spacer plate, the impeller hood, a flat plate, an O-ring, and the lower impeller. Lay the parts out in order as you disassemble them so that you'll be able to put the assembly together properly. Clean the parts thoroughly with a mild detergent solution, and if any parts are worn, replace them with new ones made for the dishwasher. Replace any seals, such as the O-ring or other washers, with new ones. Then reassemble the pump, being careful to keep the parts in order.

On some dishwashers, the lower impeller serves as a drain pump. This type of system usually has a reversible motor; machines with nonreversible motors have drain valves, as detailed above. If your machine has this impeller pump system and the water will not drain from the dishwasher, clean the lower pump impeller; this may solve the problem. Otherwise, call a professional service person.

Motor. If the dishwasher motor malfunctions, don't try to fix it yourself; call a professional service person to make repairs or replace the motor. Before you call for service, though, check to make sure that the timer is working and that the dishwasher is receiving power. Check for a blown fuse or tripped circuit breaker at the main entrance panel or at a separate entrance panel; if the dishwasher is portable, make sure that it's plugged in, and that the wall outlet, if it's controlled by a switch, is turned on.

Disposers

Disposers, of all the modern kitchen gadgets, are one of the closest to "indispensable." They are very sturdy, reliable units, as breakdown- and maintenance-free as any household appliance can be, and problems can usually be traced to a bone stuck in the grind wheel of the disposer. Most jams can be broken free with a piece of dowel rod, a broom handle, or a piece of 1×2. And if serious problems occur, the disposer can be replaced for less than $100.

Caution: Before doing any work on the disposer, make sure the power to the disposer is turned off.

Power. If the disposer doesn't run, first check to make sure it's receiving power. Most disposers plug into a wall outlet; make sure plug, cord, and outlet are all functioning properly. After checking these components, press the reset button on the motor housing of

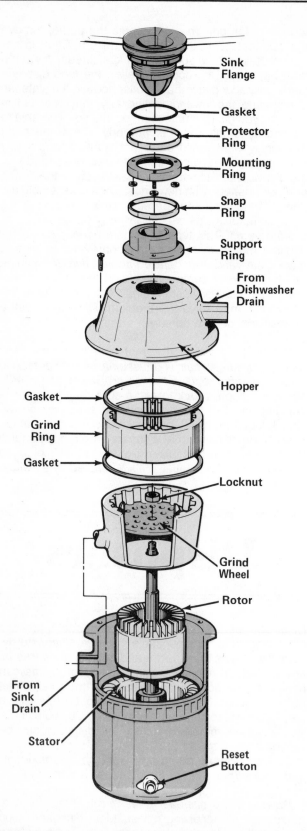

Sink Flange

Gasket

Protector Ring

Mounting Ring

Snap Ring

Support Ring

From Dishwasher Drain

Hopper

Gasket

Grind Ring

Gasket

Locknut

Grind Wheel

Rotor

From Sink Drain

Stator

Reset Button

Garbage disposers use a grind wheel driven by a motor to grind up food waste. Most problems can be traced to a piece of bone or other debris stuck in the grind wheel.

the disposer. This button is a motor overload protector; it is usually red, and is marked "reset." If necessary, wait a few minutes and press the button again. If the disposer continues to stop or hum after the reset button has been pushed several times, check the grind wheel for blockage, as below. If the disposer has been running hard for a period of time, let the motor cool for 30 minutes before you press the reset button.

If the reset doesn't reactivate the motor, check for blown fuses or tripped circuit breakers at the main electrical entrance panel; if necessary, restore the circuit. If the circuit is receiving power, the wall switch may be faulty. Test the switch with a voltage tester. Take off the switch cover plate; place one probe of the tester on one terminal and the other probe on the other terminal. If the tester bulb lights, the switch is functioning; if it doesn't light, the switch is faulty. Replace the switch with a new one of the same type; connect the wires exactly the same way they were connected to the old switch. *Caution: Make sure the power to the circuit is turned off before you replace the switch.*

Some disposers have a switch on the motor housing, located near the terminal housing box. When this type of disposer is installed, this switch is often wired to the wall switch for convenience. Check this switch to make sure it's in the "on" position.

Hums, Grinds, and Sticks. Turn off the power *immediately* when the motor starts to hum instead of spinning the grinding mechanism. The overload protector on the motor will usually break the circuit—but not always.

Humming is usually the result of a bone or a piece of metal or glass stuck on the grind wheel of the grinder. Poke a broom handle or a piece of sturdy dowel or 1×2 into the grind wheel, against one of the hammers. Try to break the grind wheel free with the handle. If this doesn't work, turn off the power. *Caution: You must turn off the power to the unit before following this procedure. At the main entrance panel, remove the fuse or trip the circuit breaker that controls the circuit; if you aren't sure which one this is, remove the main fuse or trip the main circuit breaker to turn off the power to the entire house. Before you go ahead, test the disposer again to make absolutely sure the power is off.*

With the power off, reach into the grinder and feel for obstructions on top of the grind wheel next to the housing. If you feel an obstruction, try to remove it with pliers, a piece of wood, gloved fingers, or an old fork or knife. Try turning the wheel again with the broom handle to provide leverage. *Do not* use a steel pry bar; this could damage the disposer. If you can remove the obstruction, turn on the power; then turn on the water and the disposer and let the unit run for a couple of minutes to flush away any debris.

The grind wheel hammers—or impeller blades, as they are sometimes called—can cause the grinding wheel to bind and the motor to hum. If the problem is not an obstruction, turn the power to the disposer off, as above. *Caution: Do not proceed until you're absolutely sure the power is off.* Reach into the disposer and try moving the hammers or impellers. If they feel locked against the housing or feel broken or damaged, they will have to be replaced. This is not a tough job, but it takes patience. Leave the power turned off.

To make the repair, remove the unit from the mounting screws on the sink, and unscrew all hose and wire connections to the disposer. Then remove the holding screws that lock the unit to the bottom of the sink opening. On top of the unit are several screws or bolts that hold the housing of the grinder to the motor assembly; remove these screws or bolts. This opens the grinder housing so that the grind wheel the hammers are fastened to can be removed.

On some disposers, the hammers can be removed; on others, the hammers are part of the grind wheel, and the grind wheel must be replaced. As you disassemble the disposer, make a list or a drawing of how the parts go together, so that you'll be able to reassemble the unit properly.

While the unit is disassembled, check the grind wheel for sharpness. If it feels dull—and you've noticed that the disposer works slowly — replace this part with a new one. Also check the area below the grind wheel for dirt, and clean it if necessary; waste falls into this part, and can sometimes slow the operation of the disposer. Finally, reassemble the disposer with the new parts needed, and turn on the power.

Leaks. Since water and tubing are involved in the operation of a disposer, many small problems can develop that will choke the disposer or cause it to leak. The problem is finding the leak, because the water may travel a considerable distance before it becomes noticeable. *Caution: Before working on the disposer's water system, turn off the water supply to the disposer. Also make sure the power to the disposer is turned off.*

First, if the disposer is connected to a dishwasher, check the clamp that holds the dishwasher hose to the disposer. A dishwasher drainage system through the disposer is under pressure, and the dishwasher pump can put considerable strain on the hose, causing it to leak. Hot water from the dishwasher can deteriorate the hose.

The hose clamp is usually a metal strap clamp like those found on auto radiator hoses. Turn the clamp screw to tighten the clamp. If this treatment doesn't work, check the hose; if it's cracked or worn, replace the hose with a new one of the same type. Unscrew the clamps at the disposer and in back of—or underneath at the back of—the dishwasher. Slide the clamps up the hose and disconnect the hose, and twist the hose to break the connection. Install the new hose the same way the old one was attached; make sure the connections are secure.

The drainpipe of the disposer is usually connected to

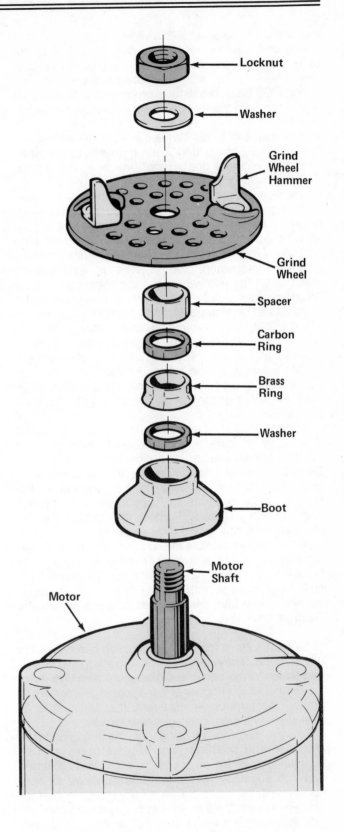

On some disposers, the hammers can be removed; on others, the hammers are part of the grind wheel, and the entire grind wheel assembly must be replaced.

the side of the disposer with a slip-joint nut, similar to a U-trap on a lavatory or kitchen sink. This joint is another potential leak point. To stop a leak at this joint, first tighten the nut with channel-lock pliers or a pipe wrench. Go easy; these tools produce lots of leverage, which can strip the threads. If tightening doesn't work, disconnect the pipe, and either wrap the pipe threads with joint tape or cover the male threads (never female) with pipe joint compound. Then reassemble the pipe.

If this treatment doesn't stop the leak, the pipe is probably split or broken, or the threads on the pipe connection are badly worn or stripped. In this case, you'll have to replace the pipe. You may need additional information on making pipe repairs; if necessary, consult a book on plumbing. Disconnect the pipe and take it to an appliance or plumbing retailer to make sure the replacement pipe fits perfectly. Also look for leaks under the floor where the drainpipe connects to the main drain. If you find a leak at this point, call a professional service person or a plumber.

Leaks can occur around the sink flange of the disposer, because the spin of the grind wheel can force water up and past this seal. To stop a leak at the flange, tighten the nuts on the mounting bolts, or, if the disposer is designed this way, the bolts. This usually stops the leak. If this doesn't work, disconnect the disposer from the mounting flange.

Some disposers have a mounting flange and sealing washer; others have a rubber gasket that fits between the sink and the flange, or a plumbers' putty seal instead of a rubber gasket. There is usually a mounting ring, with two or more bolts that hold the unit to the flange. As you disconnect it, support the bottom of the disposer with your hand. Remove the old gasket or the putty and install a new gasket of the proper type and size. Finally, reassemble the unit and turn on the water.

What appears to be a leak at the faucet may actually be water splashing into the disposer. To prevent the splashing, make sure the rubber or fiber insert plug is pushed firmly into the disposer opening before the water is turned on.

Clogs. Clogs in the disposer's piping can cause the unit to grind. They can also cause backups, flooding, and leaks. When pulverized garbage doesn't go down the drain and the hopper of the disposer fills and won't empty, the problem — assuming that the grinder is working — is a clog in the disposer pipes.

To solve the problem, disconnect the drainpipe at the disposer and the first joint beyond the trap; use channel-lock pliers or a pipe wrench. With a drain-and-trap auger, clean out the drainpipe past its connection with the main drain—usually no more than six feet. Reconnect the trap section and test the system. If the disposer still doesn't work, call a professional service person. *Caution: Do not put chemical drain cleaners into the disposer in an attempt to clean the drainpipes.*

Noise and Vibration. Most disposers make noise as the grinders operate. Newer units are specially mounted to reduce this noise by reducing vibration, but don't expect absolute quiet. Excessive noise and vibration can be caused by loose mounting bolts; tighten the bolts to solve the problem.

Debris stuck in the grind wheel can also cause noise, whether it's metal (knife, spoon, fork), glass (broken china or glass), or bone, or a damaged or broken impeller or hammer. You can usually solve the problem fairly simply. First, remove the rubber or fiber insert plug from the disposer opening. *Caution: You must turn off the power to the unit before following this procedure. At the main entrance panel, remove the fuse or trip the circuit breaker that controls the circuit; if you aren't sure which one this is, remove the main fuse or trip the main circuit breaker to turn off the power to the entire house. Before you go ahead, test the disposer again to make absolutely sure the power is off.*

With the power off, reach into the grinder and feel for obstructions; if you feel an obstruction, try to remove it, as detailed above. If you can't locate any foreign matter, use a broom handle or a sturdy dowel or 1×2 to try to unstick the grinder. If the grind wheel spins, the grind wheel hammers may be damaged; in this case, replace the hammers, as detailed above.

If none of these procedures stops the noise, or vibration is still a problem, listen carefully to the disposer's motor; damaged motor bearings can cause quite a rumble. If you suspect motor trouble, don't try to fix the motor yourself; disconnect the disposer and take it to a professional service person.

Motor. Disposer motors cause few problems. They are sealed units, either split-phase or capacitor-start, encased in a metal/plastic housing. If the disposer is receiving power and the motor doesn't work, test the motor with a VOM, set to the R × 1 scale. If the meter registers zero, the overload switch is probably faulty, and the motor should be replaced. Remove the disposer from the sink and take it to a professional service person; or replace the disposer.

Also look for trouble in the terminal box. If the terminals are loose or dirty, lack of power may be caused by a poor connection. Turn off the power to the unit and disconnect the terminals. Buff them shiny with fine steel wool, then replace the terminals and screw them on tight.

Motor malfunctions may also be caused by frozen motor bearings, a faulty relay and starting capacitor, burned-out motor windings, or a worn motor seal. Do not try to correct any of these conditions; disconnect the disposer and take the entire unit to a professional service person. Before having repairs made, compare the cost of the repair with the price of a new disposer. You may be better off replacing the disposer with a new one.

Disposer Troubleshooting Chart

Caution: *Disconnect power and water before inspecting or repairing.*

PROBLEM	POSSIBLE CAUSE	SOLUTION
Unit doesn't run	1. No power.	1. Check power cord, plug, switch, and outlet. Make sure motor is plugged in. Check for blown fuses or tripped circuit breakers at main entrance panel; restore circuit.
	2. Motor overloaded or safety shutoff faulty.	2. Press reset button on control panel.
	3. Wiring loose or broken.	3. Clean and tighten terminal connections at power inlet.
	4. Motor faulty.	4. Check motor leads for proper connections. Remove motor and take to a professional, or replace motor.
Motor hums but doesn't run	1. Machine overloaded.	1. Remove part of garbage.
	2. Motor grind wheel stuck.	2. Turn power off; insert dowel or broom handle into disposer and try to free jammed grind wheel.
	3. Grind wheel hammer loose.	3. Tighten grind wheel hammer.
Disposer floods	1. Drain line or pipe clogged.	1. Run disposer intermittently, or remove hoses and clear pipes with drain-and-trap auger.
	2. Not enough slope in drain line.	2. Adjust slope in drain line to 1 inch per 4 feet of run.
Disposer coughs out garbage	1. Machine overloaded.	1. Remove part of garbage.
	2. Insert plug incorrectly positioned.	2. Adjust insert plug position.
	3. Sink seal faulty.	3. Tighten flange sink, or replace seal.
Water leaks	1. Hose loose or damaged.	1. Tighten hose connections; if hose damaged, replace.
	2. Drain nut loose.	2. Tighten drain nut.
	3. Sink seal faulty.	3. Tighten sink flange, or replace seal.
Noisy operation	1. Flange mounting nuts too tight.	1. Loosen mounting nuts slightly.
	2. Hard object jammed in grinder.	2. Remove object.
Excessive vibration	1. Flange mounting nuts too tight.	1. Loosen mounting nuts slightly.
	2. Motor bearings worn.	2. Call a professional; or remove motor and take to a professional.
	3. Grind wheel worn or clogged.	3. Replace grind wheel.

Dryers

Most dryers operate from their own power supply lines of 220-240 volts. These electrical supply lines are sometimes fused through a separate electrical entrance panel rather than through the main panel. This separate panel is located in the basement or crawl space, or in some other inconspicuous location in your home. Most dryers are vented to the outside and are grounded; gas dryers are connected to a gas line.

Very simply, a dryer consists of a large drum, into which wet laundry is loaded. A motor with pulleys, connected by a series of belts, turns the drum, and air heated by a gas heater or electric heating element is blown through the drum to dry the laundry. The temperature and speed of the drum are controlled by a series of thermostats operated from a timer device on the control panel of the dryer. As a safety device, a dryer usually has a door switch that activates the working parts. Unless the door is properly closed, the dryer won't work, regardless of the control settings on the control panel. Many dryers are equipped with a reset button on the control panel. If the motor won't run, let the dryer cool for about 10 minutes; then push the reset button. If there are no problems with the motor, switches, or electrical system, this should restart the dryer.

Caution: Before doing any work on the dryer, make sure it's unplugged. Disconnect the grounding wire. If the dryer is gas-fueled, close the gas supply valve to shut off the unit's gas supply.

Cleaning. Besides drying clothes, dryers also remove lint. This fine, fuzzy material can cause trouble, because it blocks dryer lint traps, clogs vents, and fills blowers. Lint can also gather around and in the tracks of the drum rollers, or in and under the pulleys and the drive belt. The result is poor clothes drying or, sometimes, no drying. To avoid lint problems, clean out the dryer's lint trap system every time you use the dryer.

To clean the lint screen, remove it from the unit. The screen may be located near or under the door sill, or in the top of the dryer near the control panel; it can usually be removed by pulling it up and out of its housing. Remove the accumulated lint to clear the screen; then replace the screen.

The exhaust vent also collects lint, and vent maintenance involves cleaning the lint from a screen in the dryer's vent exhaust collar and/or at the end of the exhaust vent where it sticks out through a basement window or through an exterior wall. To clean the screen, remove the clamp that holds the vent to the collar, or back out the screws that hold the vent to the collar, or pull the vent straight off an extended collar.

Clean the screen thoroughly and then replace it in the vent assembly.

To clean the vent itself, bend the end of a wire hanger into a fairly tight hook. Insert the wire into the vent and pull out any lint deposits. Also check the vent run to make sure that the vent piping or tubing isn't loose at the joints, or, in the case of flexible plastic venting, isn't sagging between hanging brackets. Breaks or sags cause undue strain on the dryer's blower system, and can cause drying problems. If the vent pipe or tubing has become clogged with lint, remove the lint by pushing a garden hose or a drain-and-trap auger through the vent to a convenient joint, and disassemble the joint to remove the debris. With this procedure, it isn't necessary to disassemble the entire vent run to determine where the blockage is.

Lint can also get into pulley grooves and roller wheel tracks inside the dryer. Even though the lint traps are cleaned regularly, open the back of the dryer cabinet once a year and vacuum up the dust and lint inside. If the roller wheel tracks are filled with lint, disassemble the cabinet and clean the tracks — especially around the idler arm — with a wood manicure stick; or use the tip of a pencil, with the lead removed, to clean the tracks, grooves, and other recesses. If the wheels look worn — they're usually nylon, plastic, or composition material — replace them with new ones of the same type.

Door Gaskets. The door of the dryer is sealed with one or more gaskets to prevent the cool air in the laundry area from being sucked into the dryer, and the hot air in the dryer from escaping. A deteriorated or damaged gasket greatly lowers the efficiency of the dryer. To check the gasket, hold a sheet of tissue paper near the rim of the door while the machine is running; if the door leaks, the paper will flutter. If the gasket or seal looks worn or warped, and has chunks of material missing or feels hard and nonresilient, it should be replaced.

Some doors, called plug-type doors, are made in two sections; the plug is equipped with a soft rubber gasket. This type of gasket is secured with gasket cement. Some plug-type glass doors have two seals, one on the door and another between the outer and inner sections. Gasketing on this type of door is more or less permanent, but it should be checked occasionally for wear and hardness.

To replace a gasket, buy a gasket made specifically for the model dryer you own. Install the new gasket as detailed in the section on gaskets in "Basic Appliance Repair Principles."

Door Switch. This component is critical to the dryer's operation; if the switch is not working, the dryer will not run unless there's a special grounding problem somewhere in the system. If such a grounding problem occurs, the dryer will run even when the door is open;

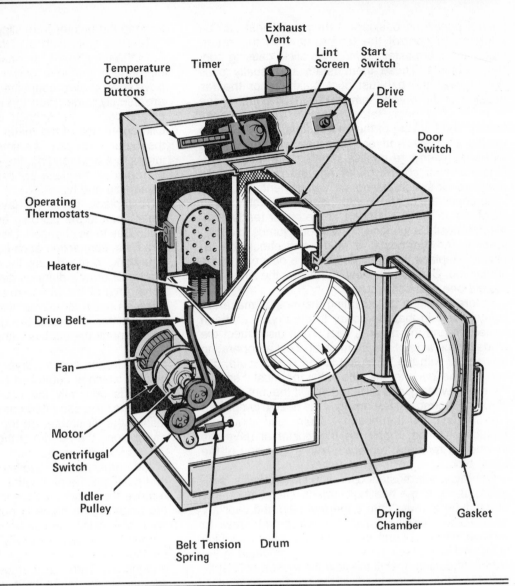

Exhaust Vent

Temperature Control Buttons

Timer

Lint Screen

Start Switch

Drive Belt

Door Switch

Operating Thermostats

Heater

Drive Belt

Fan

Motor

Centrifugal Switch

Idler Pulley

Belt Tension Spring

Drum

Drying Chamber

Gasket

*A dryer consists of a large drum, into which wet laundry is loaded.
A motor with pulleys, connected by a series of belts, turns the drum.
Air heated by a gas heater or electric heating element is blown through the drum to dry the laundry.*

in this case call a professional service person.

If the dryer has a door latch, make sure the latch is free from dirt or lint and properly adjusted before you make any switch tests or replacements. Sometimes a misaligned latch prevents the door from being closed tightly, and this in turn prevents the switch from being activated.

The switch on the dryer may be accessible from the outside door, or you may have to remove the top of the dryer to get at it. The switch is a simple assembly, with two lead wires running to it. Test the switch with a VOM, set to the R × 1 scale. The VOM should read zero; if the needle jumps, the switch is faulty, and should be replaced. Replace the switch with a new one of the same type.

The switch is held to the dryer with setscrews; remove these screws and disconnect the leads to the switch. Install a new switch and connect the leads; then position the switch and tighten the setscrews to hold it in place.

Start Switch. This switch, located on the control panel, is usually the push-button type. Start switches don't fail often, but it does happen. To check the start switch, remove the control panel and test the switch with a VOM, set to the R × 1 scale. If the meter reads zero, the switch is working; if the needle jumps to a high reading, the switch is faulty, and should be replaced. Replace the switch with a new one of the same type; connect the new switch the same way the old one was connected.

Thermostats. Thermostats, the dryer's temperature control switches, are controlled by the temperature inside the dryer, or by the heat of the motor. A temperature control switch, such as those found on dryer control panels, is basically a thermostat that can be adjusted to control the temperature in the dryer. Operating thermostats sometimes stick, causing control problems. These thermostats are usually positioned near the exhaust duct bulkhead or the fan housing of the dryer. Remove the back panel of the dryer to get at them. Before you make any checks, try tapping the housing of the thermostats lightly with the handle of a screwdriver. This may jar the contacts loose. Temperature control switches are located behind the dryer control panel, and the panel must be removed for switch testing, or replacement.

To check the control panel thermostat, test it with a VOM, set to the R × 1 scale. If the meter reads zero, the thermostat is working; if the needle jumps to a high reading, the thermostat is faulty, and should be replaced. Replace the thermostat with a new one of the same type. Connect the new thermostat the same way the old one was connected.

Before checking an operating thermostat, make absolutely certain that the power to the dryer has been turned off and the dryer is cool. Then disconnect the leads to one side of the thermostat. Test an operating thermostat with the VOM, set to the R × 1 scale; disconnect the leads to one side of the thermostat so that the meter won't give a false reading. If the meter reads zero, the thermostat is working; if the needle jumps to a high reading, the thermostat is faulty, and should be replaced. Do not repair the thermostat or have the thermostat repaired; replace it with a new one of the same type.

Operating thermostats open and close circuits, supplying power to the heating element. The components of this type of switch are a thermal bulb and capillary tube, a bimetallic disc, a switch, and a control screw. To remove this type of unit, pry out the thermal bulb, which is located in the back part of the dryer, mounted in the exhaust housing. Install the new thermostat so that its bulb fits tightly on the inside of the housing; otherwise, the bulb could collect lint. Connect the new thermostat in the same position and in the same way as the old one.

Timer. The dryer timer, located in back of the control panel, controls several things: the drying time of the clothes in the drum, the flow of electricity to the heating element, and the flow of power to the timer motor and the drum motor in the dryer cabinet. Timers are driven by synchronous motors. Although the contact part of the timer can be cleaned and adjusted on some dryers, this is a job for a professional repair person; timer motor repairs should also be handled by a professional. But you can replace a faulty timer yourself.

To get at the timer, remove the front of the control panel. On some dryers the timer can be removed without removing the panel. In either case, pull the timer knob off the shaft, and slip off the pointer. The pointer is usually keyed to the shaft by two flat surfaces to keep the pointer from slipping when it's turned.

Test the timer with a VOM set to the R × 1 scale. Turn the timer to the "normal dry" setting, and disconnect one of the timer power leads. Some timers may have several wires connected to them; the power leads are usually larger than the other wires, and this size difference can be spotted under close examination. Clip one probe of the meter to each timer terminal. If the meter reads zero, the timer is working; if the needle jumps to a high reading, the timer is faulty, and should be replaced. Replace the timer with a new one of the same size and type.

To replace the timer, have a helper hold the new timer close to the old one, especially if there are several wires to be changed. Disconnect the old wires one at a time, connecting each corresponding new wire as you work, to make sure the connections are properly made. Or draw a diagram detailing the proper connections. After all the wires are connected, check the connections again for correctness.

The timer is held to the dryer with hex-type screw bolts; unbolt the old timer and secure the new one.

Gas Heater. In a gas dryer, heat is provided by a gas heater, which is controlled by an air shutter. The gas heater is generally the source of no-heat or drying problems. You can often correct such problems by adjusting the air shutter on the gas burner, which is located along the bottom of the dryer.

To adjust the shutter, turn a thumbscrew at the end of the burner, or turn two screws in a slot and bracket that positions the air shutter. Take out the screws and remove the panel that covers the gas flame. Turn on the dryer so the flame is burning. If the flame has a deep blue color and you hear air whistling around the burner, the air/gas mixture is receiving too much air. If the flame has a yellow tip, the mixture is not receiving enough air. Turn the thumbscrew, or loosen the two screws slightly, to cut down the air to the burner. Keep turning until the flame is a light blue color, without any yellow, and the whistling stops.

The gas heater on a dryer has a pilot light to provide ignition when the gas is turned on. The pilot is a small open flame fed by a steady flow of gas. A correctly adjusted pilot flame is steady and blue, and between ¼ and ½ inch high. If the pilot flame goes out repeatedly, it may be getting too little air; if it's noisy, it's getting too much air. To correct either condition, turn the pilot adjustment screw slightly, as directed by the dryer manufacturer.

When a pilot goes out, relighting it is simple. If there is a gas valve at the pilot, turn the valve to "off" and wait at least three minutes to let any built-up gas dissipate; after three minutes, turn the valve to "pilot." If there is no safety or reset button or gas valve, simply hold a lighted match to the pilot orifice.

If the pilot flame won't stay lit after several tries, it should be adjusted by a professional; don't try to adjust

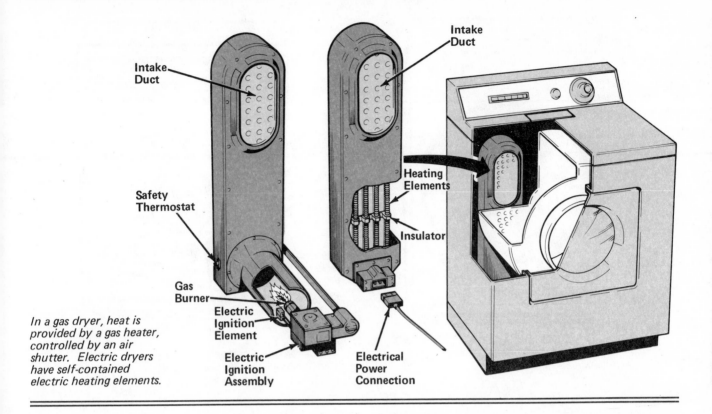

Intake Duct

Intake Duct

Intake Duct

Safety Thermostat

Heating Elements

Insulator

Gas Burner

Electric Ignition Element

Electric Ignition Assembly

Electrical Power Connection

In a gas dryer, heat is provided by a gas heater, controlled by an air shutter. Electric dryers have self-contained electric heating elements.

the mechanism or tamper with the gas line. If the dryer has a thermocouple, however, the problem may be a faulty thermocouple. You can replace this component to correct the problem, as detailed below.

Thermocouple. The thermocouple operates as a safety device, to turn off the gas supply to the dryer when the pilot light goes out. It consists of a heat sensor connected to a solenoid; when the sensor is not heated by the pilot flame, the solenoid closes the gas supply line. When the thermocouple fails, the pilot light won't stay lighted; the thermocouple may be burned out or broken. A faulty thermocouple should be replaced.

To replace a thermocouple, unscrew the copper lead and the connection nut inside the threaded connection to the gas line. Under the mounting bracket at the thermocouple tube, unscrew the bracket nut that holds the tube in place. Insert a new thermocouple into the hole in the bracket, steel tube up and copper lead down. Under the bracket, screw the bracket nut over the tube. Push the connection nut to the threaded connection where the copper lead connects to the gas line; make sure the connection is clean and dry. Screw the nut tightly into place, but do not overtighten it. Both the bracket nut and the connection nut should be only a little tighter than hand-tightened.

Electric Ignition System. Newer gas dryers use an electric ignition device rather than a pilot light to light

the gas heater. In this electric ignition system, an element becomes hot and glows like the filament in a light bulb. These electric systems are always sealed; you can't adjust or repair them. If an electric ignition device fails, call a professional service person.

Electric Heating Elements. These components, found in electric dryers, are self-contained units located in the back of the dryer. A defective heating element is frequently the source of no-heat or drying problems. Remove the back service panel to gain access to the elements.

The heating elements are located inside the heater ducts. If you think the heating element is faulty, test it with a VOM, set to the R × 1 scale. The meter should read about 12 ohms; if the reading is higher than 20 ohms, the heater is faulty, and should be replaced. A heater connected to a 115-volt line usually has an 8.4-ohm resistance; a heater connected to a 230-volt line usually has 11 ohms resistance. Replace a faulty heater with a new one of the same type and electrical rating.

The heater may also malfunction because it's grounded. To test for this set the VOM to the R × 1 scale, and remove the leads to the heater. Clip one probe of the VOM to a heater terminal and touch the other probe to the heater housing. The meter needle should jump to a fairly high reading; if the needle flicks back and forth at a low reading, the heater is probably grounded, and should be replaced.

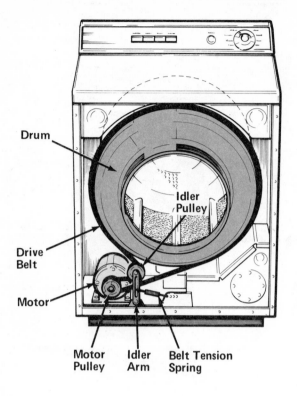

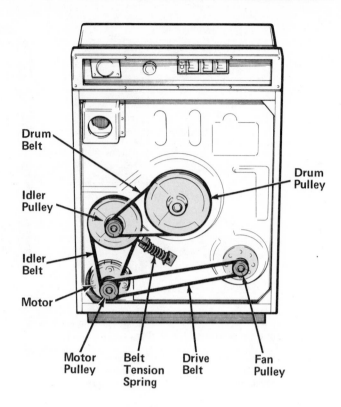

When replacing a belt (left), you may have to prop up the drum to keep it from sagging.
Some dryers (right) use a series of belts to spin the tub instead of just one.

To replace the heater, you may have to remove the cabinet top as well as the back. Disconnect the leads and remove the screws that hold the duct in position; then lift the entire heater unit out of the dryer. Once the heater is out, remove the screws that hold the heating element in the duct. Slip the new heating element into the heating duct the same way the old one came out. Be careful not to damage the resistance coils. Replace the screws that hold the heating element in the duct, reconnect the leads, and screw the unit back into position.

Fan. The most common dryer fan problem is lint clogging the air passages through the heater and through the dryer drum. To clear a clogged air passage, remove the back service panel of the dryer and back out the screws holding the air duct in place. Then reach into the duct and remove all the lint and dirt possible. Reassemble the parts.

Also inspect the fan for a loose screw connection where the motor shaft is set on the dryer's drum. Remove the back service panel, tighten the screw, and replace the panel.

Drum Belt. The drum of the dryer is usually turned by a motor and belt assembly. There are two very clear signs that the belt is malfunctioning: you can easily spin the drum by hand, or you hear a heavy thumping sound coming from the drum when the dryer is running. To get at the belt, remove the back or front service panel. Depending on the type of dryer you own, you may have to prop up the drum to keep it from sagging. Don't let the drum hang; the bolts that hold it in the cabinet could be ruined. Don't remove any more parts than you have to in order to reach the belt.

The old belt may be threaded around the idler pulley and motor drive shaft. Draw a diagram showing how the pulley is installed, so you'll be able to replace it properly. Then move the idler pulley forward, providing slack in the old belt. Remove the old belt from the pulleys, and stretch a new belt—made especially for the dryer—into place. If the old belt is worn or frayed, but not broken, leave it around the drum as a pattern for positioning the new belt; cut the old belt and remove it when the new belt is in position. The new belt must extend around the dryer drum and the pulleys. The trick here is to align the belt on the drum with the pulleys; the ribs on the new belt should go against the drum.

When the belt is aligned, turn the drum by hand, if possible, to make sure the belt is tracking. You may have to reassemble part of the cabinet to do this.

Some dryers — especially older models — have a V-belt pulley drum drive. With this system, two pulleys of different sizes are used to set the speed of the drum. To change this type of belt, decrease the tension on the idler pulley and install the new belt in the V-grooves of all pulleys. Then place the idler pulley back into position.

Drum Bearings. With the back service panel off, check the drum bearing around the dryer drum shaft. You may have to remove the dryer belt to reach it. If the bearing looks worn and dirty, or if it's loose, it should be replaced with a new bearing made for the dryer. A screw in the center of the drum connects the shaft to the drum; remove this assembly and then lift off the drum pulley. Support the drum to prevent it from sagging. The bearing fits around the drum shaft, and is slip-fit. Pull off the old bearing and install the new one; secure it the same way the old one was held. On some dryers, the bearing and shaft are held by a U-bolt, and there are two tapered blocks supporting the bearing and shaft. Remove the bearing by first removing the U-bolt and blocks.

When reassembling the bearing unit, make sure the parts go back together the way they came apart. If the part is assembled with shims, the shims could be placed between the bearing and the support channels. Do not overtighten the screws holding the parts; overtightening could cause damage to the bearing. If the bearing has a lubrication wick, saturate it with auto transmission oil.

Drum Rollers. The front of the dryer's drum is usually supported by two rollers. These wheels are either metal with a rubber rim or pressed nylon. If the rollers squeak, but appear to be in good condition, apply a few drops of No. 20 nondetergent motor oil — not all-purpose oil — to them. If the rollers are worn, you can replace them if the roller assembly is not riveted.

First, remove the front of the cabinet. Rollers are usually held on a metal shaft by a spring clip. To remove the roller, pry the spring clip off with a screwdriver. Under the clip are a washer, the roller, and another washer. You might have to remove a small nut at the back of the shaft, and remove the shaft, in order to reach the roller. Remove the roller from the shaft, and clean away built-up lint and dirt before installing the new roller. This dirt and lint buildup could cause the drum to turn slowly, preventing proper drying and straining other dryer components. Put the new roller on the shaft with the washers in the same position.

Motors. Motor malfunctions usually call for service by a professional. There are three main causes of motor failure, and it is recommended that you check these trouble spots before you call a professional service person or take the motor to a repair shop: lack of lubrication, defective motor switch, or worn or frozen bearings.

Humming can be related to a burned-out motor or a defective switch. Remove the back access panel. Then reach behind the drum, motor pulley, and idler arm pulley. If these areas are clogged with dirt and lint, undue strain on the motor may be causing the humming noise. Worn or broken belts can also cause a humming noise. Check the belts for wear and damage, and replace them if necessary, as detailed above. If the belts look all right, you may be able to stop the noise by spraying them with fan belt dressing, available at automotive and hardware stores and home centers.

Next, turn the dryer on. The noise you hear may be the whirl of the spinning drum, not the motor. Some noise is normal.

Most motors are permanently lubricated and sealed by the manufacturer; access to the bearings is not possible. However, force a little No. 20 nondetergent motor oil—not all-purpose oil—around the ends of the motor shaft; this lubrication may stop the humming noise. If this doesn't solve the problem, remove the motor and take it to a professional service person.

The centrifugal switch on the dryer motor may be located on top of the motor. Humming, no motor power, and no heat can be caused by a faulty centrifugal switch. If the switch is externally mounted, check the terminals of the switch to make sure they are tight and not burned. If you spot trouble, remove the switch and take it to a professional service person for testing; the switch will probably have to be replaced. Some centrifugal switches are located inside the motor housing; you won't be able to remove the switch. In this case, remove the entire motor and take it to a professional for repairs.

If the motor hums, but won't run the pulley on the end of the motor shaft, try turning the pulley by hand. *Caution: Before turning the pulley, make sure the power to the dryer is turned off.* If you can't turn the pulley, or the pulley is very hard to turn, the bearings in the motor may be worn. Remove the motor and take it to a professional service person for repairs, or replace the motor. Replacement may be cheaper than repair.

Some motors have overload protectors, which turn off the motor when excess strain is put on it. Often, dryers are equipped with a reset button on the control panel. If the motor won't run, let the dryer cool for about 10 minutes and then press this reset button. The dryer may operate; if it doesn't, check for an overload protector on the motor.

Test the overload protector with a VOM, set to the R × 1 scale. If the meter reads zero, the protector is working; if the needle jumps to a high reading, the overload protector is faulty, and should be replaced. Remove the protector by prying it off or unscrewing it from the motor housing. Replace it with a new one of the same size and type; connect the new protector the same way the old one was connected.

Dryer Troubleshooting Chart

Caution: Disconnect power and fuel before inspecting or repairing.

PROBLEM	POSSIBLE CAUSE	SOLUTION
Dryer doesn't run	1. No power.	1. Check power cord, plug, and outlet. Check for blown fuses or tripped circuit breakers at main entrance panel or at separate panel; restore circuit.
	2. Motor overloaded or safety shutoff faulty.	2. Press reset button on control panel.
	3. Controls not properly set.	3. Set controls properly.
	4. Door not closed.	4. Close door so switch activates drum.
	5. Wiring loose or broken.	5. Clean or tighten terminal connections at power inlet.
	6. Door switch faulty.	6. Remove lint and dirt from switch orifice; make sure switch is making contact. Test switch; if faulty, replace.
	7. Door hinges broken or misaligned.	7. Repair hinges so that switch makes contact; if hinges damaged, replace.
	8. Timer faulty.	8. Make sure timer is properly set. Test timer; if faulty, replace.
	9. On/off switch faulty.	9. Make sure switch is properly set. Test switch; if faulty, replace.
	10. Motor faulty.	10. Check motor leads for proper connections. Remove motor and take it to a professional, or replace motor.
	11. Centrifugal switch faulty.	11. If accessible, check switch terminal connections. If inaccessible, call a professional. Or remove switch or entire motor and take to a professional.
Fuses blow	1. Grounding faulty.	1. Call a professional.
	2. Motor bearings worn.	2. Call a professional, or remove motor and take to a professional.
Dryer doesn't heat	1. Inadequate power supply.	1. Check fuses and switches to make sure 220-volt power is being supplied; half of double-fuse hookup may be blown. If necessary, restore circuit.
	2. Lint blockage.	2. Clean lint screen; clean air duct.
	3. Thermostat faulty.	3. Lightly tap thermostat housing to jar contacts loose. Test thermostat; if faulty, replace.

Dryer Troubleshooting Chart (Continued)

PROBLEM	POSSIBLE CAUSE	SOLUTION
Dryer doesn't heat (continued)	4. Timer faulty.	4. Make sure timer is properly set. Test timer; if faulty, replace.
	5. Overheat protector faulty.	5. Test leads; if faulty, replace. If switch is located inside motor, call a professional.
	6. Centrifugal switch faulty.	6. If accessible, check switch terminal connections. If inaccessible call a professional. Or remove switch or entire motor and take to a professional.
	7. Electric heating element faulty (electric units).	7. Test heating element; if faulty, replace.
	8. Gas heater faulty (gas units).	8. Check to make sure pilot is lit; if necessary, relight. Adjust air shutter of gas burner.
	9. Thermocouple faulty (gas units).	9. Replace thermocouple.
	10. Electric ignition faulty (gas units).	10. Call a professional.
	11. No gas (gas units).	11. Call gas company.
	12. Motor faulty.	12. Check motor leads for proper connections. Remove motor and take to a professional, or replace motor.
Drying slow or inadequate	1. Machine overloaded.	1. Reduce size of load.
	2. Clogged lint screen.	2. Clean lint screen.
	3. Clothes not adequately wrung out.	3. Make sure spin cycle on washer is spinning clothes dry.
	4. Vent blocked.	4. Clean vent. Make sure vent is not sagging, bent, broken at joints, clogged, or loose where it joins dryer's vent collar.
	5. Door seal defective.	5. Check door for air leaks. Check and tighten gasket screws; if gasket faulty, replace.
	6. Blower faulty.	6. Clean blower assembly; check and tighten blower bolts.
	7. Thermostat faulty.	7. Lightly tap thermostat housing to jar contacts loose. Test thermostat; if faulty, replace.
	8. Timer faulty.	8. Make sure timer is properly set. Test timer; if faulty, replace.

Dryer Troubleshooting Chart (Continued)

PROBLEM	POSSIBLE CAUSE	SOLUTION
Drying slow or inadequate (continued)	9. Electric heating element faulty (electric unit).	9. Test heating element; if faulty, replace.
	10. Belt sticking, worn, or broken.	10. Clean belt and pulleys. Check belt; if worn or damaged, replace.
	11. Drum seal faulty.	11. Check drum seals at front and back of drum; if faulty, call a professional.
	12. Exhaust fan clogged or jammed.	12. Clean fan assembly. Check for frozen bearings by turning; if necessary, lubricate.
Drum doesn't turn	1. Belt misaligned or broken.	1. Adjust or replace belt.
	2. Drum bearings need lubrication.	2. If possible, lubricate bearings.
	3. Exhaust fan needs lubrication.	3. Lubricate fan assembly.
Light won't go on	1. Bulb burned out.	1. Replace bulb.
	2. Door switch faulty.	2. Test switch; if faulty, replace.
Motor runs when door is open	1. Door switch faulty.	1. Remove lint and dirt from orifice; make sure switch is making contact. Test switch; if faulty, replace.
Noisy operation	1. Metal or plastic object in drum.	1. Remove foreign objects from drum. Noise from buttons and clips on clothing is normal.
	2. Duct clogged or out of position.	2. Clean duct, if necessary, reposition.
	3. Belt sticking, worn, or broken.	3. Clean belt and pulleys. Check belt; if worn or damaged, replace.
	4. Pulleys misaligned.	4. Realign pulleys.
	5. Rollers sticking or damaged.	5. Lubricate or replace rollers.
	6. Exhaust fan needs lubrication.	6. Lubricate fan assembly.
	7. Motor bearings worn or need lubrication.	7. Lubricate motor shaft ends. Call a professional, or remove motor and take to a professional, or replace motor.
	8. Centrifugal switch faulty.	8. If accessible, check switch terminal connections. If inaccessible, call a professional. Or remove switch or entire motor and take to a professional.

Ranges and Ovens

Ranges and ovens operate fairly simply, and they're usually easy to repair, mainly because the components are designed for quick take-apart. Most of the malfunctions that affect gas ranges involve the supply and ignition of gas in the burners and the oven; most of the problems that affect electric ranges involve faulty heating elements.

Caution: Before doing any work on a range or oven, make sure it's unplugged, or turn off the electric power to the unit by removing a fuse or tripping a circuit breaker at the main entrance panel or at a separate panel. If there is a grounding wire to the range, disconnect it. Also close the gas supply valve to shut off the unit's gas supply.

Fuses. If an electric range or oven is receiving power, but doesn't work, the unit may have its own fuse or circuit breaker assembly. This assembly is usually located under the cooktop of the range. Inside the oven, look back to spot the fuse assembly. In some units, lift the top of the range to gain access to the fuse assembly; or lift the elements, remove the drip pans, and look toward the sides of the cabinet.

If the unit has this additional fuse or breaker system, components such as the oven light, the range heating elements, the timer and a self-cleaning feature may be separately fused. If these components or features fail

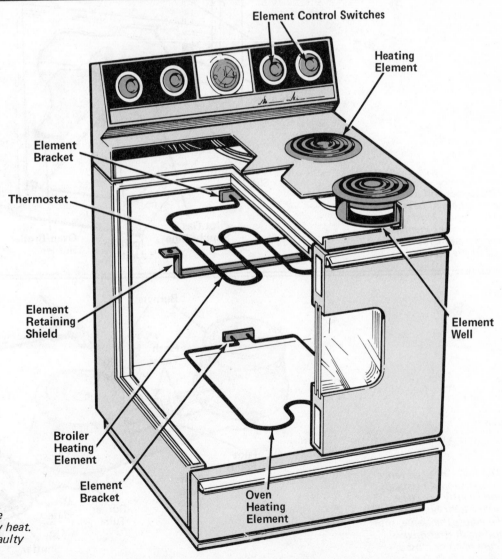

Element Control Switches

Heating Element

Element Bracket

Thermostat

Element Retaining Shield

Element Well

Broiler Heating Element

Element Bracket

Oven Heating Element

Electric ranges and ovens use nichrome elements to supply heat. Most malfunctions involve faulty heating elements.

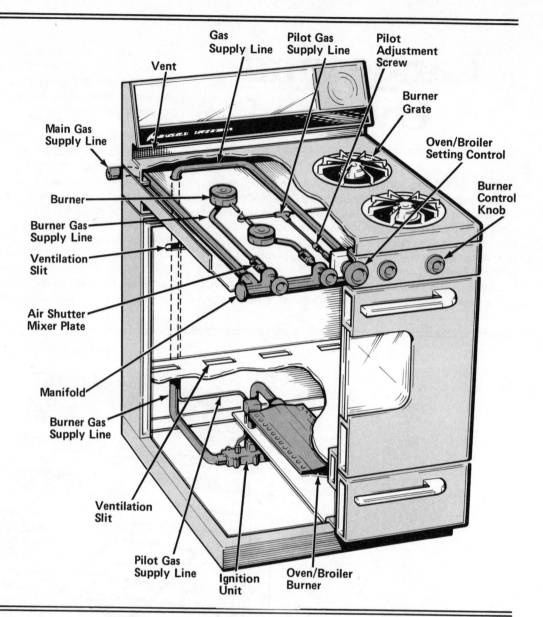

Vent

Gas
Supply Line

Pilot Gas
Supply Line

Pilot
Adjustment
Screw

Burner
Grate

Oven/Broiler
Setting Control

Burner
Control
Knob

Main Gas
Supply Line

Burner

Burner Gas
Supply Line

Ventilation
Slit

Air Shutter
Mixer Plate

Manifold

Burner Gas
Supply Line

Ventilation
Slit

Pilot Gas
Supply Line

Ignition
Unit

Oven/Broiler
Burner

Gas ranges and ovens use gas burners to heat and cook food. Most malfunctions involve the supply and ignition of gas in the burners.

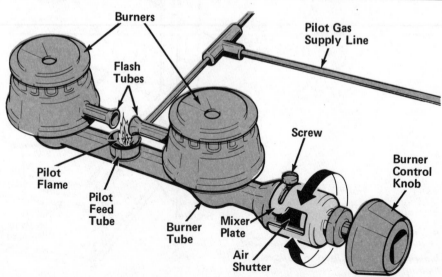

Burners

Flash
Tubes

Pilot Gas
Supply Line

Screw

Burner
Control
Knob

Pilot
Flame

Pilot
Feed
Tube

Burner
Tube

Mixer
Plate

Air
Shutter

The flame of a gas range burner should be steady and slightly rounded, with a light-blue tip. To adjust the flame, slide the air shutter mixer plate open or closed.

to work, don't overlook the possibility that the fuses have blown. To replace a blown fuse, unscrew the old fuse and install a new one of the same type and electrical rating. *Caution: Do not use a fuse with more than a 15-amp rating.* If the unit has circuit breakers, push the breaker or reset button to activate the circuit. This reset button is usually found on the control panel.

Gas Range Burners. Clogged burners are a very common problem with gas ranges, because food spilled on the burners blocks the gas ports and prevents ignition. On some gas ranges you can remove the top ring of the burner to expose the ports. With a cloth moistened with water and household detergent, clean the burner. Then, with a straight pin or needle, clean out the gas ports. *Caution: Do not use a toothpick or matchstick to clean the gas ports. If the tip of the wood gets stuck in the burner ports, it could cause a serious blockage.*

If the burner is thickly encrusted with burnt food, turn off the power supply, both gas and electric, to the range; then remove the burner. Soak the burner in a solution of mild household detergent and water, and then clean the burner with a soft cloth. Clear the gas ports with a pin or needle, rinse the burner, and let it dry. When the burner is completely dry, replace the burner and turn on the power and the gas supply.

The flame of gas range burners should be steady and slightly rounded, with a light blue tip. The flame should be quiet, and should respond to adjustments made at the control knobs. Most burner troubles can be quickly solved by adjusting the air shutter mixer plate, which is located at the end of the burner tube near the knob controls. Turn a small screw on the plate and slide the plate open or closed; then tighten the setscrew. If the flame is yellow, it's not receiving enough air; open the plate slightly. If the flame is high, or makes a roaring noise, it's getting too much air; close the plate slightly.

Burner Switches. The switches that control the burners of a gas range are similar to the oven thermostat; there is a sensing bulb connected to the switch. If you suspect a switch is faulty, don't try to fix it yourself; remove it from the range and take it to a professional. The bulb is usually clipped to the range cabinet; pry it off with a screwdriver. Take the entire unit to a professional service person for testing; if the switch is faulty, replace it with a new one made for the range. Connect the new switch the same way the old one was connected.

If the range can be adjusted to control the simmer setting at the burners, you can make this adjustment by removing the control knob to the burner. Inside the knob shaft, locate a screw slot. Turn this screw, usually counterclockwise, and test the burner. If it doesn't work properly, turn the screw clockwise and test the burner again. Repeat this procedure until the setting is correct.

Electric Range Heating Elements. When a range heating element burns out, it's easy to replace. But before any disassembly to check or replace an element, make sure the range is receiving power. First check the power cord, the plug, and the outlet; then look for blown fuses or tripped circuit breakers at the main entrance panel or at a separate panel. Finally, check the fusing system inside the range. If the circuit is broken, restore it; if the range is receiving power, go on to check the element.

In most ranges, each top heating element is connected to a terminal block in the side of the element well. To get at the terminal block, lift the element and remove the metal drip pan that rests below it. The element is held by two retaining screws or is push-fit into the terminal block. To remove a screw-type element, remove the screws holding the wires. To remove a push-type element, pull the element straight out of its connection.

Test the element with a VOM set to the R × 1 scale. If the element is functioning properly, the meter will read between 40 and 125 ohms; if the meter reads extremely high, the element is faulty and should be replaced.

To test a range element without a VOM, remove a working element from its terminal block and connect it to the malfunctioning element terminal. Don't let the test element overlap the edges of the element well; keep the element inside the well, even if it doesn't fit perfectly. Then turn on the power to the range. If the working element heats, the suspected element is bad, and should be replaced. If the working element doesn't heat, chances are the terminal block wiring or the switch that controls the element is faulty. In this case, call a professional.

Replace a burned-out range element with a new one made specifically for the range. Take the old element to the appliance parts store to make sure you get the right type; if possible, take the make and model information, too. This data will probably be on a metal tag attached to the back service panel of the range. To install the new element, connect it the same way the old one was connected.

Element Switches. When an element doesn't work, the problem may be the element or the element switch. Procedures for element replacement are detailed above. A faulty element switch cannot be repaired; call a professional service person for replacement.

Pilot Lights. One pilot light usually serves all the top burners of a gas range; on some ranges there are two pilot lights, one for each side of the range. A correctly adjusted pilot flame is steady and blue, between ¼ and ½ inch high. If the flame goes out repeatedly or if it's yellow at the tip, it's getting too little air; if there's a space between the flame and the pilot feed tube, it's getting too much air. To correct either condition, turn

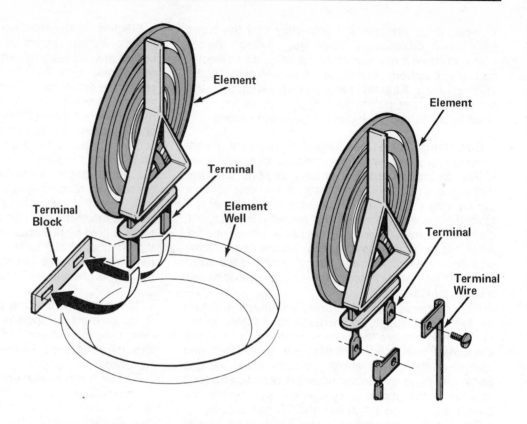

To remove a range heating element, remove the screws holding the terminal wires, or pull the element straight out of its connection.

the pilot adjustment screw on the gas line slightly, as directed by the manufacturer of the range.

When the pilot goes out, relighting it is simple. If there is a gas valve at the pilot, turn the valve to "off" and wait at least three minutes to let any built-up gas

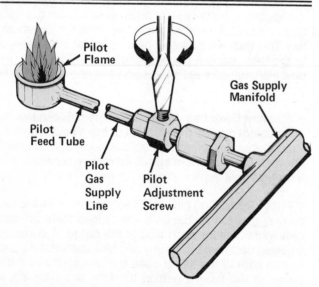

To adjust the pilot flame, turn the adjustment screw on the gas line, as directed by the range manufacturer.

dissipate; after three minutes, turn the valve to "pilot." If there is a safety or reset button, push the button, and keep it depressed. Hold a lighted match to the pilot orifice, and turn the gas valve to "on"; then, when the pilot is burning brightly, release the reset button. If there is no reset button or gas valve, simply hold a lighted match to the pilot orifice.

If the pilot flame won't stay lit after several tries, it should be adjusted by a professional; don't try to adjust the mechanism or tamper with the gas line. If the range has a thermocouple, the problem may be a faulty thermocouple. You can replace this component to correct the problem, as detailed below.

If the pilot flame is properly adjusted but the flame doesn't ignite the burners, the problem is probably in the flash tubes that run from the pilot to the burners. These tubes may be blocked by spilled food from the burners. If this is the case, turn off the power to the range, and then, with a short piece of wire, clean out the tubes. Push the wire through the opening until the tube is clear; you may have to disconnect the tube to clear it. After cleaning the tube, replace it in the same position.

If the pilot has a switch, the switch may be faulty. Turn off the power to the range, and test the switch with a VOM, set to the R × 1 scale. If the switch is functioning, the meter will register zero; if the meter reads higher than zero, the switch is faulty, and should be replaced. Remove the switch and replace it with a new one of the same type; connect the new switch the same way the old one was connected.

The oven pilot light is usually located toward the back of the oven, or under the bottom panel of the oven box. If the range has a drawer unit under the oven, pull out the drawer; this may help you locate the pilot. If the oven doesn't light, the oven pilot may be out or may be set too low. If the pilot is out, relight it, as above. If the flame is set too low, adjust it. Next to the pilot, locate a small box-like unit with a couple of screws in it. This is the ignition unit. The ignition unit could also be located below the pilot; follow the gas line down until you locate the ignition unit. Turn one of these screws on the ignition. Experiment, turning the screws a little at a time, until the flame is adjusted properly. It should not be as high as the top pilot flame; leave it as low as possible. On some oven pilots, turn the control to "off" and light the pilot; then turn the oven dial to "broil."

Thermocouple. On some gas ranges, the pilot assembly includes a thermocouple, a safety device that turns the gas supply off when the pilot light goes out. The thermocouple consists of a heat sensor connected to a solenoid; when the sensor is not heated by the pilot flame, the solenoid closes the gas supply line. When the thermocouple fails, the pilot light won't stay lighted; the thermocouple may be burned out or broken. A faulty thermocouple should be replaced.

To replace a thermocouple, unscrew the copper lead and the connection nut inside the threaded connection to the gas line. Under the mounting bracket at the thermocouple tube, unscrew the bracket nut that holds the tube in place. Insert a new thermocouple into the hole in the bracket, steel tube up and copper lead down. Under the bracket, screw the bracket nut over the tube. Push the connection nut to the threaded connection where the copper lead connects to the gas line; make sure the connection is clean and dry. Screw the nut tightly into place, but do not overtighten it. Both the bracket nut and the connection nut should be only a little tighter than hand-tightened.

Automatic Shutoff Valve. On some gas ranges, there is an automatic shutoff in the pilot assembly; this valve shuts off the gas to the burner any time the pilot and the burner are both off. If this unit malfunctions, don't try to fix it yourself; call a professional service person for repair or replacement.

An electrically operated shutoff valve used on some gas ranges has two facing valves, an electromagnet, and a manually activated reset button. The thermocouple fitting is next to the pilot valve, as in most burner systems. A small amount of electricity is generated in the thermocouple, and this electricity holds the facing valves apart. If the pilot light goes out, no electricity is generated, and the valve closes to turn the gas off. On this type of system, relight the pilot by depressing the reset button and holding a match to the pilot. It takes about a minute to light this pilot. If you aren't able to relight this system, call a professional service person.

Electric Ignition System. Most newer gas ranges and ovens don't have pilot lights; instead, the gas is ignited by an electric ignition system. In this type of system, an element becomes hot and glows like the filament in a light bulb when an electric current passes through it. The heat from the filament lights the gas. As a rule, these ignition systems are sealed; they cannot be repaired or adjusted. When an electric ignition device fails, don't try to fix it; call a professional service person for replacement.

Oven Door Gasket. If the oven won't heat to the desired temperature or heats unevenly, the problem could be a defective door gasket. The best way to test for this is to pass your hand around the door, being careful not to touch it, while the oven is turned on. If you can feel heat escaping, the gasket needs replacement. Replace it with a new gasket made for the range.

On most ovens, the gasket—made of asbestos—is located on the frame of the oven, and the door closes against it. This gasket is generally friction-fit in a channel, and can be replaced. In other units, the oven door is in two sections, and the gasket is not mounted on the door frame, but installed between the front and back sections of the door. Don't try to replace this type of gasket; call a professional service person.

To replace a frame-mounted gasket, pull the old one out of the channel, and then clean the channel and the door frame with a solution of mild household detergent and water. To install the new gasket, start the replacement at the top of the door frame and work down the sides; ease the gasket around corners. Finish the installation along the bottom; butt the ends of the gasket firmly together. On some oven door frames the gasket is held in place with screws. To get at the screws, bend back the exposed edge of the gasket.

Oven Setting Control. When this component, located on the control panel, malfunctions, the oven won't heat. To remedy the situation, remove the control knob. Then remove the back service panel or the front panel, if necessary. Remove other control knobs as needed to remove the panel. The oven setting control is located directly in back of the control knob, and is usually held to the control panel by two screws. Testing the control with a VOM is not recommended, because the results will not always be conclusive. The best procedure is to substitute a control that you know is working, if you suspect that the setting control is faulty. Or simply replace the faulty control with a new one made for the oven. Disconnect the electrical lead wires from the control terminal and lift out the control. Connect the new control the same way the old one was connected.

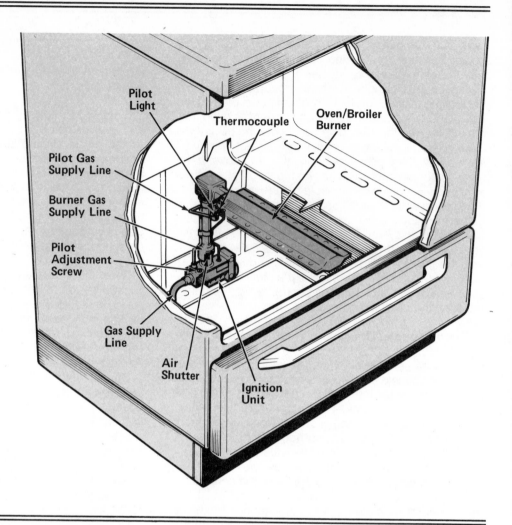

Pilot Light

Thermocouple

Oven/Broiler Burner

Pilot Gas Supply Line

Burner Gas Supply Line

Pilot Adjustment Screw

Gas Supply Line

Air Shutter

Ignition Unit

The oven pilot is usually located at the back of the oven; turn a screw on the pilot ignition unit to adjust the pilot flame height.

Timer. The range timer is usually located in the control panel on top of the range. If you suspect the timer is faulty, don't try to fix it yourself; remove it and take it to a professional service person for testing. To take out the timer, remove the back service panel to the control panel and release the spring clips that hold it in position, or remove the retaining screws. Then push the timer forward to release it. Then remove the electrical lead wires from the timer housing.

If, when disassembling the timer, you notice that the electrical wire terminals look burned, remove these leads and buff the leads and the terminal points with fine steel wool. Burned and/or dirty terminals can cause the timer to malfunction; cleaning can solve this problem.

Replace the old timer or install a new one of the same size and type, if this is necessary. Connect the new timer the same way the old one was connected.

Oven Thermostat. If the oven doesn't heat evenly, or doesn't heat at all, the oven thermostat may be malfunctioning. First, determine how much the temperature in the oven is off from the control setting. Put an oven thermometer inside the oven and turn the oven on for about 20 minutes, with the thermostat set at 350° F. Or set the oven at any range between 300° and 400° F. If the oven thermometer reads 25° or more lower or higher that the oven control setting, the thermostat should be recalibrated.

To calibrate the thermostat on some ranges, pull off the thermostat knob on the control panel. Behind the knob are two screws holding a round, notched plate. Loosen these screws, but do not remove them. With a screwdriver, change the notch setting on the notched plate by turning the plate counterclockwise; for every eighth of a turn, the oven temperature goes up about 25° F. To turn the heat down, move the plate clockwise.

Some thermostats can be adjusted by turning a screw inside the control knob shaft housing. To do so, remove the knob and insert a screwdriver into the shaft so that the screwdriver blade engages a screw slot. Turn the screwdriver counterclockwise about one-eighth of a turn to raise the heat about 25° F.

If a malfunctioning thermostat cannot be recalibrated, it should probably be replaced. Test the thermostat with a VOM, set to the R × 1 scale. If the thermostat is in working order, the meter will register zero; if the needle jumps to a higher reading, the thermostat is faulty, and should be replaced. Replace the thermostat with a new one of the same type.

First disconnect the terminal wires to the thermostat and pull off the control knob. The thermostat is usually held to the control panel with retaining screws. On some ranges, there is a wire running from the thermostat into the oven. This wire operates a sensing bulb that controls the thermostat. The sensing bulb is usually held by a bracket; unscrew this bracket to remove the bulb. Then carefully slip out the wire, the bulb, and the thermostat. Install the new thermostat in reverse of the way the old one came out.

Oven and Broiler Heating Elements. Electric oven and broiler elements are often even easier to test and replace than range elements. If the oven element doesn't work, first check to see if the range is receiving power; don't overlook the fusing system inside the range. If the range is receiving power, set the timer on the range to "manual." If the element still doesn't heat, turn off the power to the range, and test it with a VOM, set to the R × 1 scale.

The oven and broiler heating elements are connected almost the same way as the range elements. Remove the screws or plugs that connect the element to the power. Remove a retaining shield, which is usually held by two screws, and remove the element from the brackets that hold it in the oven. The element is usually held in these brackets by screws. If the element is in working order, the meter will read from 15 to 30 ohms. If the meter reads higher than 30 ohms, the element is faulty, and should be replaced. If the element tests all right but doesn't work, the problem may be at the terminals; make sure the terminals are clean and tight at the element connections.

Oven and broiler elements cannot be tested without a VOM. If you don't have a VOM, take the element to a professional service person for testing. The problem is usually a malfunctioning element, however; you aren't risking much by replacing the element without a professional test.

Replace a burned-out element with a new one made specifically for the oven or broiler. Take the old element to the appliance parts store to make sure you get the right type; if possible, take the make and model information, too. To install the new element, place it in the same position as the old one. Connect it the same way the old one was connected, and use the same screws to hold it in place.

Self-Cleaning Ovens. These are two types of self-cleaning ovens, pyrolytic and catalytic. Pyrolytic ovens use very high heat — usually 1,000° F — to incinerate food on the oven's surface; catalytic ovens, also called continuous-clean ovens, are coated with a special

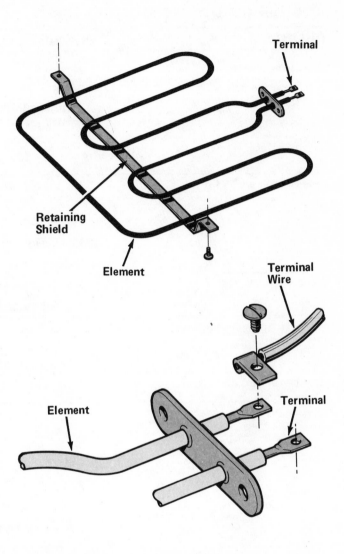

To remove an oven or broiler heating element, remove the screws or pull the plugs that connect it. Remove a retaining shield and lift out the element.

finish that allows most dirt to burn away at normal cooking temperatures. *Caution: Never use a commercial oven cleaner to clean any part of either a catalytic or a pyrolytic oven.*

Most problems with pyrolytic ovens occur because procedures are not properly carried out. In most cases, the oven heat selector must be set to "clean," and the oven door must be firmly closed and, sometimes, latched. When the oven reaches a predetermined temperature—about 600° F—the door automatically locks shut so that it can't be opened during the cleaning cycle. If you've followed the correct procedures for using a self-cleaning oven but the oven is not coming clean, call a professional service person.

Gas Range Troubleshooting Chart

Caution: *Disconnect power and fuel before inspecting or repairing.*

PROBLEM	POSSIBLE CAUSE	SOLUTION
No burners light	1. No gas.	1. Make sure gas valve is open. If valve open, call gas company.
	2. If range has electric ignition, no power.	2. Check power cord, plug, and outlet. Check for blown fuses or tripped circuit breakers at main entrance panel or at separate entrance panel; restore circuit.
One burner won't light	1. No gas to burner.	1. Test other burners; if they light, clean burner assembly.
	2. Pilot light out.	2. Relight pilot.
	3. Electric ignition faulty.	3. Call a professional.
	4. Defective gas valve.	4. Call gas company.
Pilot won't stay lit	1. Pilot light set too low.	1. Adjust pilot light.
	2. Gas feed tube blocked.	2. Clean feed tube.
Burners pop when lighted	1. Conduction tubes misaligned.	1. Reposition conduction tubes on holding bracket.
	2. Pilot light set too low.	2. Adjust pilot light.
Light won't go on	1. Bulb burned out.	1. Replace bulb.
Oven won't heat	1. No gas to range.	1. Make sure gas shutoff valve is open. If valve is open, call gas company.
	2. Defective gas valve.	2. Call gas company.
	3. Pilot light out.	3. Relight pilot.
	4. Pilot light set too low.	4. Adjust pilot light.
	5. Electric ignition system faulty.	5. Call a professional.
	6. Thermostat faulty.	6. Test thermostat; if faulty, replace. If thermostat inaccurate, recalibrate; if no result, call a professional.
	7. Timer faulty.	7. Clean timer terminals; set timer to "manual" and turn clock on control panel 24 hours ahead. If no result, call a professional.
Oven heat uneven	1. Door gasket faulty.	1. Make sure door is closed tightly and hinges operate smoothly; if gasket damaged, replace, or call a professional.
Burner won't simmer	1. Simmer nut needs adjustment.	1. Adjust simmer nut on burner.
Flame yellow	1. Not enough air in gas mixture.	1. Adjust air shutter.
Flame noisy	1. Too much air in gas mixture.	1. Adjust air shutter.
Flame too high	1. Too much air in gas mixture.	1. Adjust air shutter.

Gas Range Troubleshooting Chart (Continued)

PROBLEM	POSSIBLE CAUSE	SOLUTION
Soot forms on burner	1. Air shutter clogged. 2. Air shutter needs adjustment.	1. Clean air shutter. 1. Adjust air shutter.
Gas smell	Leave the house immediately; do not try to turn off the gas, or turn any lights on or off. Go to a telephone and call the gas company or the fire department immediately to report a leak. Do not reenter your home.	

Electric Range Troubleshooting Chart

Caution: Disconnect power before inspecting or repairing.

PROBLEM	POSSIBLE CAUSE	SOLUTION
No elements heat	1. No power.	1. Check power cord, plug, and outlet. Check for blown fuses or tripped circuit breakers at main entrance panel or at separate panel, and in range fuse system. Restore circuit.
One element won't heat	1. Element faulty. 2. Switch faulty. 3. Terminal block wiring faulty.	1. Test element; if faulty, replace. 2. Call a professional. 3. Call a professional.
Element heats slowly or does not get red-hot	1. Inadequate power supply. 2. Element connections faulty. 3. Element faulty.	1. Check fuses and switches to make sure 220-volt power is being supplied; half of double-fuse hookup may be blown. If necessary, restore circuit. 2. Clean and tighten element connections. 3. Test element; if faulty, replace.
Element heats but food does not cook well	1. Pan not resting flat on element.	1. Use flat-bottomed pan.
Elements burn out often	1. Inadequate power supply. 2. Foil covering pan below element.	1. Check fuses and switches to make sure 220-volt power is being supplied; half of double-fuse hookup may be blown. If necessary, restore circuit. 2. Make sure drip pans below elements are not covered by aluminum foil.
Light won't go on	1. Bulb burned out.	1. Replace bulb.
Oven won't heat	1. No power. 2. Oven element faulty. 3. Control switch faulty.	1. Check power cord, plug, and outlet. Check for blown fuses or tripped circuit breakers at main entrance panel or at separate panel, and in range fuse system. Restore circuit. 2. Test element; if faulty, replace. 3. Call a professional.

Electric Range Troubleshooting Chart (Continued)

PROBLEM	POSSIBLE CAUSE	SOLUTION
Oven won't heat (continued)	4. Timer faulty.	4. Clean timer terminals; set to "manual" and turn clock on control panel 24 hours ahead. If no result, call a professional.
Broiler doesn't work	1. No power.	1. Check power cord, plug, and outlet. Check for blown fuses or tripped circuit breakers at main entrance panel or at separate panel, and in range fuse system. Restore circuit.
	2. Broiler element faulty.	2. Test element; if faulty, replace.
	3. Control switch faulty.	3. Call a professional.
	4. Timer faulty.	4. Clean timer terminals; set to "manual" and turn clock on control panel 24 hours ahead. If no result, call a professional.
Oven temperature uneven	1. Door gasket faulty.	1. Make sure door is closed tightly; if gasket damaged, replace or call a professional.
	2. Thermostat faulty.	2. Test thermostat; if faulty, replace. If thermostat inaccurate, recalibrate; if no result, call a professional.
Timer won't work	1. Terminals loose or corroded.	1. Clean and tighten terminals; if no result, call a professional.
Element smokes and smells	1. Food spills; soap residue.	1. Clean element and drip pan with steel-wool soap pad; some odor is normal after cleaning.

Refrigerators and Freezers

Refrigerators and freezers, like air conditioners, consist of two basic components — a condenser coil and an evaporator coil. A liquid coolant is circulated through these coils by a compressor and a motor. The refrigerant liquid is cooled in the condenser; it then flows to the evaporator. At the evaporator, the air in the unit is cooled by contact with the liquid-filled coil. The condenser of a refrigerator or freezer is the coil on the outside of the unit; the evaporator is the coil on the inside. The coolant is circulated through the system by a compressor.

The unit's compressor system, which forces the coolant through the coil system, is driven by a capacitor-type motor. Other basic parts of the cooling/defrosting system include switches, thermostats, heaters, condensers, and fans. You can test and replace many of these refrigerator components. However, there are exceptions, as noted in the procedures below, which are best left to a professional.

Caution: Before doing any work on a refrigerator or freezer, make sure it's unplugged. After unplugging the unit, check to see if the motor/compressor has a capacitor; this component is located in a housing on the top of the motor. Capacitors store electricity, even when the power to the unit is turned off. Before you do any work on a capacitor-type refrigerator or freezer, you must discharge the capacitor, or you could receive a severe shock.

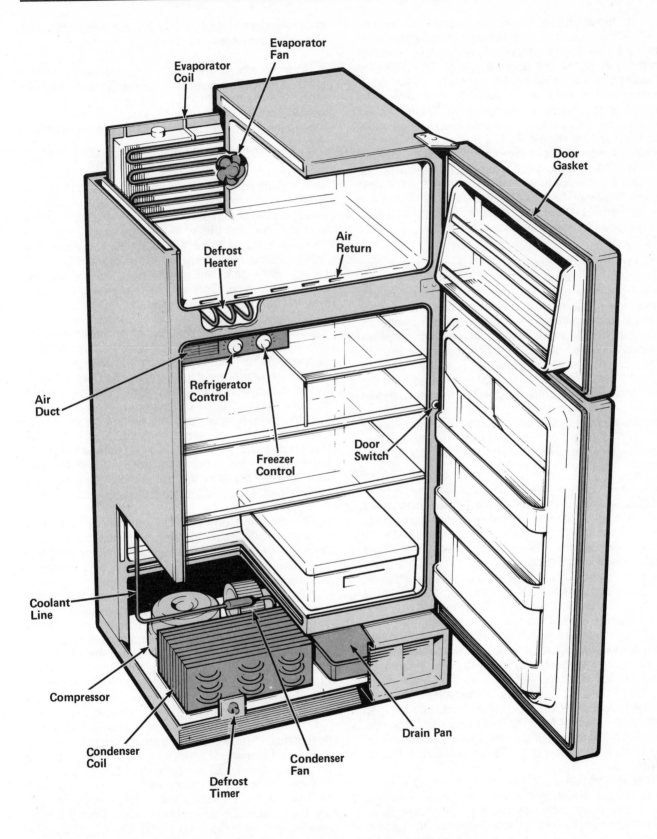

Evaporator
Fan

Evaporator
Coil

Door
Gasket

Air
Return

Defrost
Heater

Refrigerator
Control

Air
Duct

Freezer
Control

Door
Switch

Coolant
Line

Compressor

Drain Pan

Condenser
Coil

Defrost
Timer

Condenser
Fan

*In a refrigerator, coolant is cooled in a condenser; from there it flows to the evaporator,
where air is cooled by contact with the coil.*

First, unplug the refrigerator or freezer. To gain access to the capacitor, remove the service panel over the back rear portion of the unit, or the service panel on the front of the unit below the door. The capacitor is located in a housing on the top of the motor/compressor unit; it looks like a large dry cell battery. To discharge the capacitor, use a 20,000-ohm, 2-watt resistor, an inexpensive wire unit available at most electrical supply stores. Fasten the probes of the resistor to the terminals of the capacitor; this discharges the capacitor. If the capacitor has three terminal posts, connect the resistor to one outer terminal and the center terminal; then to the other outside terminal and the center terminal. After discharging the capacitor, you can proceed to make the necessary repairs.

Cleaning and Positioning. The condenser and evaporator coils of a refrigerator collect dust and dirt over a period of time. This decreases their efficiency. Thus, one of the most important maintenance procedures is to clean these coils with a vacuum cleaner, a soft cloth, and/or a whisk broom, *at least* once a year.

Positioning also affects the efficiency of the unit. Refrigerators or freezers with exposed condenser coils on the back panel should be at least two inches from the wall, and the back of the refrigerator or freezer should not be placed against a heat register or a window or door where heat or sun could affect the temperature of the coil. To keep your refrigerator or freezer working properly, make sure it is clean and well positioned at all times.

Door Gaskets. When a refrigerator gasket becomes hard or cracked, its seal is broken, and the unit's efficiency drops sharply. Test the door gasket for leaks by placing a dollar bill between the gasket and the door jamb, and closing the door. Pull the bill out. If it offers some resistance, chances are the gasket fits properly. If the bill comes right out, or falls out, the gasket is faulty, and should be replaced. Test the gasket at several locations around the door.

To replace a gasket, buy a gasket made specifically for the model refrigerator you own. If you aren't sure about the model number of your refrigerator, cut out a small section of the gasket and take the sample to an appliance dealer for matching. If the gasket has to be ordered, you can glue the section back into the gap with rubber cement for a make-do repair until the new gasket comes in. Install the new gasket as detailed in the section on gaskets in "Basic Appliance Repair Principles."

Test the gasket on a freezer door with the same dollar-bill procedure; if the gasket is faulty, replace it with a new gasket made especially for the freezer door. Do not remove the freezer door to replace the gasket. Freezer doors are often tensioned with spring devices, which can be very troublesome to replace after the

door has been removed; and on some models wiring has to be disassembled, too.

Door Switch. On the refrigerator door jamb, locate a small push-button switch. This component operates the light inside the refrigerator or freezer. If the switch is malfunctioning, the light in the unit may stay on, and the heat from the light bulb can cause cooling trouble in the box.

If you suspect the door switch is faulty, first make sure the bulb is not burned out; then depress the push button. If the light stays on, remove the switch from the jamb. Remove retaining screws hidden by a plastic trim piece, pry the switch out of the jamb with a screwdriver, or pry off the jamb trim to expose the switch. Then test the switch with a VOM, set to the R × 1 scale. The meter should read zero; if the needle on the scale moves above zero, replace the switch with a new one of the same type. Connect the new switch the same way the old one was connected.

Limit Switch. The limit switch is found only on frost-free refrigerators and freezers; its function is to keep the defrost heating element from exceeding certain set temperatures. If a refrigerator has lots of frost in the freezer compartment, the problem may be the limit switch. However, other components — the evaporator fan, the defrost timer, and the defrost heater — can cause the same problem. Check these parts for malfunctions, as detailed below. If these parts are in working condition, the problem is most likely in the limit switch. Don't try to fix the limit switch yourself; call a professional service person for replacement.

Thermostat Control. This component is usually mounted inside the refrigerator; the visible control knob is turned to regulate the refrigerator/freezer temperature. The workability of this control can be tested in various ways, depending on the problem.

If the compressor runs all the time, turn the control knob to the "off" position. If the compressor still runs, unplug the unit; then pull off the control knob and remove the screws holding the thermostat in place. Pull out the thermostat, and remove either the red or the blue wire from its terminal. Plug in the unit. If the compressor doesn't run, the thermostat is faulty; replace it with a new one of the same type. Connect the new thermostat the same way the old one was connected.

If the compressor runs after the wire is removed from its terminal, there is probably a short circuit somewhere in the unit's wiring. In this case, don't try to fix the problem yourself; call a professional service person.

If the refrigerator or freezer runs but the box doesn't cool, unplug the unit; then, with a screwdriver, remove the thermostat. Disconnect both wires from the thermostat, and tape the ends of the wires together with electrical tape. Plug in the appliance. If the refrigerator starts and runs normally, the thermostat is faulty; re-

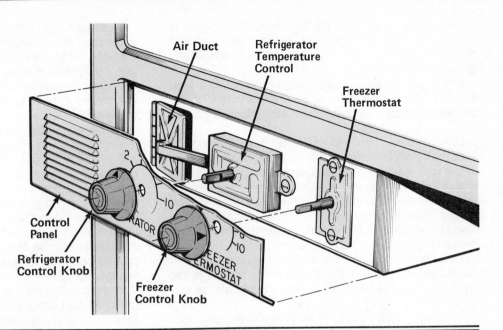

Air Duct

Refrigerator
Temperature
Control

Freezer
Thermostat

Control
Panel

Refrigerator
Control Knob

Freezer
Control Knob

The thermostat controls regulate the temperature of both the refrigerator and the freezer. Pull off the control knobs, and remove the control panel to reach the controls.

place it with a new one of the same type. Connect the new thermostat the same way the old one was connected.

If the freezer compartment is normal but the refrigerator box doesn't cool, set the dials that control both compartments to mid-range. Remove these knobs; they're usually friction-fit. Then unscrew the temperature control housing; you'll see an air duct near the control. Replace the knob on the freezer thermostat, and turn the control to "off." Open the refrigerator door and look closely at the air duct. If this duct doesn't open wider in about 10 minutes, the control is faulty; replace it with a new one of the same type. Connect the new control the same way the old one was connected.

Evaporator Fan. In some cases, a faulty thermostat may not be the cause of a warm refrigerator or freezer. A warm box may also be caused by a defective fan, a blocked fan, or broken or bent fan blades. If the blades are jammed, try to free them; if they're bent, straighten them with pliers. If this doesn't solve the problem, call a professional service person.

On some refrigerators, the door switch operates the evaporator fan; if the fan seems to be malfunctioning, the door switch could be faulty. Test the switch as detailed above, and replace it if necessary.

Defrost Timer. If the compressor doesn't run, chances are the defrost timer is malfunctioning. This part is located near the compressor. To test the defrost timer, unplug the refrigerator. Disconnect the wires from the timer and timer motor; remove the timer from its brackets by backing out two retaining screws. Test the defrost timer with a VOM, set to the R × 1 scale. Clip one probe of the VOM to each defrost timer—not

motor — wire, and turn the timer control screw shaft until it clicks. If the defrost timer is functioning, the meter will read zero. If the needle jumps, the defrost timer is faulty; replace it with a new one of the same type. Connect the new defrost timer the same way the old one was connected.

To check the defrost timer motor, clip one probe of the VOM to each motor wire, and set the scale to R × 100. If the meter reads between about 500 and 3,000 ohms, the motor is functioning properly. If the meter reads higher than 3,000 ohms, the timer motor is faulty; replace it with a new one of the same type. Connect the new motor the same way the old one was connected.

Defrost Heater. This component is a heating element located on the evaporator coil; when the refrigerator or freezer switches to the defrost cycle, the defrost heater is turned on to melt the frost in the compartment. Failure of the defrost heater causes failure to defrost.

Test the element with a VOM, set to the R × 1 scale. To gain access to the heating element, remove the compartment's wall panels. The meter should read between 5 and 20 ohms; if it doesn't, the heating element is faulty, and should be replaced. Replace the heater with a new one of the same type and electrical rating; connect the new heater the same way the old one was connected.

Condenser Fan. This component is located under the unit. If the fan is malfunctioning, the refrigerator or freezer won't cool properly, or will run continuously or not at all.

Test the fan with a VOM, set to the R × 1 scale. If the

meter reads from 50 to 200 ohms, the motor is functioning properly. If the meter reads higher than 200 ohms, the fan motor is faulty; replace it with a new one of the same type.

While you're working on the fan motor, make sure the fan blades are clean and unobstructed. If the blades are bent, straighten them with pliers.

Drain Ports. The drain ports are located along the bottom of both the freezer and the refrigerator sections of the unit. These holes can become clogged with debris or with ice, causing a drainage problem when the unit is defrosting. To clear the ports, use a short section of wire that will fit the holes. Do not use a toothpick; the wood may break off in the port. On some refrigerators, the drain ports are located near the defrost heater at the evaporator coils. A lot of disassembly is required to clean this type of unit; if the refrigerator or freezer is this type, you may be better off calling a professional service person to clear the ports.

On some freezer compartments, the drain is located under the freezer compartment, and shaped like a shoehorn. This type of drain can usually be unscrewed so that the drain area can be cleaned properly.

Ice Makers. Freezers with automatic ice makers sometimes malfunction because the water inlet valve strainer that feeds water to the ice maker becomes clogged. To correct this problem, unplug the appliance and disconnect the water supply. Then remove the water line where it enters the valve—usually at the bottom edge of the unit. Locate the wire strainers, remove them, and clean the strainers with a stiff brush and mild household detergent. Reassemble the component in reverse fashion.

Wet Insulation. When condensation appears on the outer shell of a refrigerator or freezer in a specific and confined area, the insulation inside the unit is probably wet. This problem is usually caused by moisture penetrating the insulation through a broken jamb or trim strip that covers the gap between the outer and inner shells of the unit.

To correct the problem, unplug the refrigerator or freezer and empty it. Prop the door open. Leave the unit off, with its door open, for 36 to 48 hours; this should be ample time for the insulation to dry. During this period, examine the trim strips. If you find any cracks in them, pry out the strips with the tip of a screwdriver or the blade of a putty knife, and replace them with new ones. If this treatment doesn't work, the insulation may be thin in spots. In this case, call a professional service person to replace or repack the insulation.

Wet insulation may also be due to broken shelf supports. Broken brackets also cause shelf leveling problems. The supports — metal or plastic — are easy to replace; don't try to repair them. Lift the broken support up and off its mounting bracket, and replace it with a new one of the same type.

Refrigerant Leak. Coolant leaks are identifiable by their acrid smell. There is nothing you can do to repair a coolant leak; call a professional service person to deal with the problem.

Motor/Compressor. The compressor and motor of a refrigerator or freezer are contained in a sealed unit. If you trace problems to either of these components, do not try to fix the unit yourself; call a professional service person.

Refrigerator/Freezer Troubleshooting Chart

Caution: Disconnect power before inspecting or repairing.

PROBLEM	POSSIBLE CAUSE	SOLUTION
Unit doesn't run	1. No power.	1. Check power cord, plug, and outlet. Check for blown fuses or tripped circuit breakers at main entrance panel; restore circuit.
	2. Controls not set properly.	2. Set controls properly. If no result, test controls; if faulty, replace.
	3. Compressor fan faulty.	3. Call a professional.
	4. Timer faulty.	4. Call a professional.
	5. Compressor relay faulty.	5. Call a professional.
Fuses blow	1. Circuit overloaded.	1. Put on different circuit.
	2. Voltage low.	2. Call a professional or the power company.

Refrigerator/Freezer Troubleshooting Chart (Continued)

PROBLEM	POSSIBLE CAUSE	SOLUTION
Unit doesn't cool	1. Very hot weather.	1. Set thermostat several degrees lower.
	2. Door gasket faulty.	2. Check gasket for leaks; if faulty, replace.
	3. Condenser coil dirty.	3. Pull unit away from wall and vacuum condenser coil; or remove bottom access panel and clean coil.
	4. Unit needs defrosting.	4. Defrost, reset, and test unit.
	5. Unit in bad location.	5. Move unit at least 2 inches away from wall; keep away from registers and windows.
	6. Light stays lit when door is shut.	6. Replace switch.
	7. Wet insulation around unit.	7. Take unit out of service so insulation can dry; locate and mend leak.
	8. Door doesn't close tightly.	8. Level unit so door closes by itself. Check door alignment; if necessary, reset or replace hinges.
	9. Unit overloaded.	9. Store less food in unit.
	10. Condenser fan clogged.	10. Clean fan assembly. If no result, replace if possible; otherwise, call a professional.
	11. Defrost timer faulty.	11. If timer is not complex, test and replace. If timer is complex, disconnect and take to a professional.
	12. Coolant leak.	12. Call a professional.
	13. Defrost heater faulty.	13. Call a professional.
	14. Frost on evaporator coil.	14. Defrost; then defrost frequently.
Frost forms quickly or unit doesn't defrost	1. Controls set incorrectly.	1. Reset thermostat control to higher temperature.
	2. Defrost heater faulty.	2. Test heater; if faulty, replace.
	3. Defrost limit switch faulty.	3. Call a professional.
	4. Door opened too often.	4. Open door less often.
	5. Door gasket faulty.	5. Check gasket for leaks; if faulty, replace.
	6. Door sagging.	6. Level unit so door closes by itself. Check door alignment; if necessary, reset or replace hinges.

Refrigerator/Freezer Troubleshooting Chart (Continued)

PROBLEM	POSSIBLE CAUSE	SOLUTION
Frost forms quickly or unit doesn't defrost (continued)	7. Drain clogged (frost-free unit).	7. Defrost freezer; clean drain port.
Noisy operation	1. Unit not level.	1. Level unit from front to back and side to side.
	2. Drain pan vibrating.	2. Reposition pan; if damaged or warped, replace.
Condensation	1. Controls set incorrectly.	1. Set thermostat control to higher temperature.
	2. Door opened too often.	2. Open door less often.
	3. Door gasket faulty.	3. Check gasket for leaks; if faulty, replace.
Water leaks	1. Drains clogged.	1. Defrost and clean drain ports.
	2. Drain hose cracked or split.	2. Replace drain hose.
	3. Drain pan cracked.	3. Replace drain pan.
Unit runs continuously	1. Door gasket faulty.	1. Check gasket for leaks; if faulty, replace.
	2. Controls set incorrectly.	2. Set thermostat control to higher temperature.
	3. Condenser coil dirty.	3. Pull unit away from wall and vacuum condenser coil; or remove bottom access panel and clean coil.
	4. Unit in bad location.	4. Move unit at least 2 inches away from wall; keep away from heat registers and windows.
	5. Door opened too often.	5. Open door less often.
	6. Coolant leak.	6. Call a professional.
Cycles too frequent	1. Condenser coil dirty.	1. Pull unit away from wall and vacuum condenser coil; or remove bottom access panel and clean coil.
	2. Compressor relay faulty.	2. Call a professional.
Light won't light	1. Bulb burned out.	1. Replace bulb.
	2. Door switch faulty.	2. Test switch; if faulty, replace.
Ice maker won't work	1. Blockage in strainer unit.	1. Defrost; clean strainers.
Bad smell in unit	1. Spoiled food in unit.	1. Remove spoiled food and clean unit.
	2. Drains clogged.	2. Defrost, clean drain ports.
	3. Drain pan dirty.	3. Clean drain pan.

Washers

Because they do so many things, washing machines may be harder to diagnose than to replace — mainly because of the special timing cycles that operate valves and motors that turn water on, spin the tub, drain water, and control the water temperature. But diagnosis can be done; all it takes is common sense and patience.

Caution: Before you do any work on the washer, make sure it's unplugged. Disconnect the grounding wire and the water hoses.

Basic Operating Checks. Before starting a serious appraisal, follow these procedures. First, make sure the washer is receiving power. Check the cord, the plug, and the outlet; if a wall switch controls the outlet, make sure the switch is working. Look for blown fuses or tripped circuit breakers at the main entrance panel; restore the circuit. If the unit is receiving power and still won't run, press a reset button on the control panel, if the washer has one.

Second, make sure the control knob is properly set and the door is tightly closed. Check the latch to make sure it's free of lint and soap buildup.

Third, make sure that both water faucets are turned on, and that the drain and soap-saver return hoses are properly extended, without kinks. If the washer has a water-saver button, make sure the button is depressed; water may not circulate through the filter nozzle if the basket is not full and the button is not depressed.

Finally, make sure the water is the proper temperature. Check the temperature selector switches on the control panel to make sure they're properly set. Also check the water heater temperature control; it should be set no lower than 120° F.

Cleaning. Wipe the top and door of the washer clean regularly to prevent the buildup of dirt and detergent. When you wash very linty materials, remove lint from

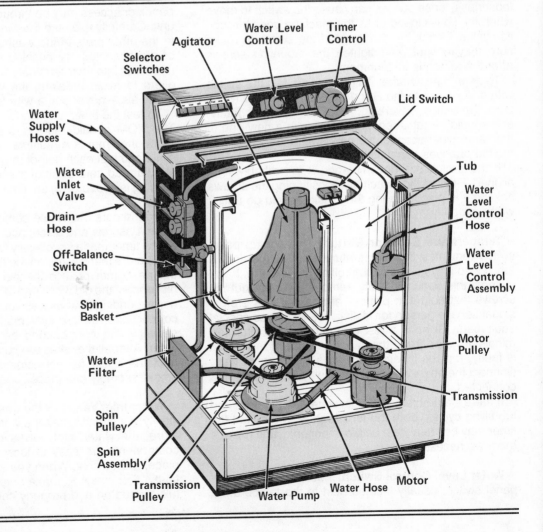

A washing machine has a tub and an agitator; various cycles operate valves and motors, turn water on, spin the tub, drain water, and control the water temperature. Problems can occur in either the electrical or the plumbing system.

Selector Switches
Agitator
Water Level Control
Timer Control
Lid Switch
Water Supply Hoses
Water Inlet Valve
Drain Hose
Off-Balance Switch
Tub
Water Level Control Hose
Water Level Control Assembly
Spin Basket
Water Filter
Motor Pulley
Spin Pulley
Transmission
Spin Assembly
Transmission Pulley
Water Pump
Water Hose
Motor

the tub after removing the laundry. Soap deposits may cause laundry to smell bad, but this problem is easy to solve. Fill the tub with water and add one pound of water softener or one gallon of white vinegar; then run the machine through the complete wash cycle. If the deposits are really bad, wash the inside of the tub with a solution of household ammonia and mild detergent. Rinse throughly and then wipe the tub with liquid bleach. *Caution: Rinse the tub thoroughly before wiping it out with bleach. Ammonia and bleach can combine to form a very dangerous gas.* Finally, run the machine through a complete wash cycle.

Lid Switch. The lid switch often serves as a safety switch; if the switch is not working, or the switch opening in the lid is clogged with detergent, the machine will not run. If you suspect a detergent block, try cleaning out the port with a wood manicure stick after the power is turned off. Clean off any detergent buildup around the rim of the lid; sometimes there's enough detergent crusted on the metal to prevent the lid from closing tightly and keep the washer from operating. If cleaning doesn't help, remove the top of the cabinet to get at the switch. With the switch exposed, check the screws for looseness; loose screws can cause the switch to move when the lid is closed or as the machine goes through its cycles. Check the terminals of the switch to make sure they're tight, and tighten the mounting screws after the switch is in alignment.

To determine whether it's functioning, test the switch with a VOM, set to the R × 1 scale. If the meter reads zero, the switch is working; if not, the switch is faulty, and should be replaced. Replace it with a new one of the same type; connect the new switch the same way the old one was connected.

If the switch still doesn't work, it is probably misaligned. Realign the switch by repositioning the screws holding it in place, testing the switch as you go until it works properly.

Temperature Selector Switch. This control panel switch regulates the temperature of the water in the tub; it also plays a role in controlling the fill cycle. If you suspect this switch is faulty, remove it — back out the screws that hold it in place — and take it to a professional service person for testing; the test takes special equipment. Or hook a test wire across the switch terminals; if water flows, the switch is faulty. If the switch is faulty, replace it with a new one of the same type. Connect the new switch the same way the old one was connected.

If there's a problem with both water temperature and tub filling cycles, both the temperature switch and the timer may be faulty; test both components, and replace them as necessary.

Water Level Control Switch. This is another control panel switch, usually located next to the temperature switch. There is a small hose connected to this switch, and sometimes this hose becomes loose and falls off the connection. When this happens, the water in the tub usually overflows. To solve this problem, cut about ½ inch off the end of the hose and reconnect it, with a push fit, to the switch. The switch itself can also malfunction, resulting in tub overflow and other water-level trouble in the tub. If you suspect this switch is faulty, remove it by backing out the screws holding it in place, and take it to a professional service person for testing. If the switch is faulty, replace it with a new one of the same size and type; connect the new switch the same way the old one was connected.

Timer. Most washing machine timers are very complicated. The timer controls most of the operations of the washer: water level, tub filling and emptying, length of cycles, and cycle setting sequences. For this reason, any repairs to the timer should be made by a professional service person. However, there are a couple of checks you can make when you suspect the timer is faulty; and you may be able to install a new timer.

To get at the timer, remove the control knobs and the panel that covers the controls. This may be a front panel, or access may be through a panel in back of the unit. Carefully examine the wires that connect the timer to the other parts of the washer. If the wires are loose or disconnected, try pushing them into position; they usually fit into their terminals like plugs. Use long-nose pliers to avoid breaking the wire connections to the terminals — never pull a wire by hand.

To test the timer, use a VOM, set to the R × 1 scale. The VOM should read zero if the timer is working. Since the timer is a multiple switch, turn it through its cycle and test each pair of terminals in turn. The meter should read zero at all of these points. If one or more reading is above zero, the timer is faulty, and should be replaced.

Most timers are single components. To replace the timer, unscrew and disconnect the old one, and install a new timer made specifically for the washing machine. If there are many wires on the timer, have a helper hold the new timer next to the old one as you work, and disconnect the old wires one at a time, connecting each corresponding new wire as you work, to make sure the connections are properly made. Or draw a diagram showing the connections before removing the old timer. After all the wires are connected, check the connections again for correctness, and then screw the timer assembly into place.

Water Inlet Valves. If the washer won't fill or fills very slowly, if it overfills, or if the water is the wrong temperature, the water inlet valves could be faulty. These components are easy to locate and very easy to replace, at little cost. When you suspect an inlet valve is faulty, first check to make sure the water faucets are fully turned on and properly connected to the hot and

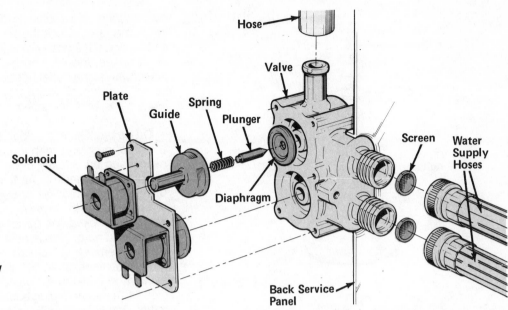

If the washer won't fill, fills very slowly, overfills, or the water is the wrong temperature, the inlet valve could be faulty. Before replacing an inlet valve, check the water connection and the valve screens. Try gently tapping the solenoids; if this doesn't work, replace the inlet valve assembly.

Hose

Valve

Plate

Guide

Spring

Plunger

Solenoid

Diaphragm

Screen

Water Supply Hoses

Back Service Panel

cold inlets of the valves. Then check the screens in the valves; if they're clogged, clean or replace them. If water doesn't enter the tub, set the temperature control to "hot." If there is no water, set the control to "warm." If all that comes out is cold water, the hot-water inlet valve is faulty. Reverse the procedure to test the cold-water valve, setting the control first on "cold" and then on "warm." If the tub overfills, unplug the washer. If water still flows into the tub, the valve is stuck open. In any of these cases, the valves should probably be replaced.

To gain access to the valve assembly, take off the back service panel and disconnect the hot- and cold-water hoses to the valves. Remove the hoses connected to the valves inside the cabinet, and also disconnect the wires from the terminals. Back out the screws holding the valves to the machine. The inlet valves have solenoids inside the housing. These can be tested, but chances are the valve is simply worn out. Try tapping the solenoid with a screwdriver handle; if this doesn't work, replace the entire inlet valve assembly — repairs usually cost more than a new part. Replace a faulty inlet valve assembly with a new one of the same type; install it in reverse of the way you disconnected the old one.

Tub and Agitator. The washing machine tub, or basket, usually doesn't cause problems, but it can cause damage to the laundry, make a lot of noise, vibrate, or stop completely.

If laundry is torn during the wash cycle, feel around the tub. If you find a rough spot, you may be able to smooth it with emery cloth. Sand lightly. If this doesn't work—or if you have to cut to bare metal to remove the roughness—the tub should be replaced, and it's prob-

ably much wiser to replace the entire washer.

The agitator—the finned part that fits on the tub shaft — can also tear laundry if the fins are cracked or broken. You may be able to solve the problem temporarily by pinching off the splinters with pliers and lightly filing the plastic smooth, but this is just a stopgap measure; the agitator should be replaced. Replace a damaged agitator with a new one of the same type. To do this, unscrew the cap on top of the agitator. With the cap off, pull straight up on the agitator; it should lift off. If it doesn't move, rap its side with a hammer. If it still won't lift off, drive wedges under the bottom rim of the agitator to dislodge it. Then set the new agitator into place and replace the agitator cap.

Damage to the snubber, a pad-like device sometimes located under the agitator cap, can cause the machine to vibrate. The snubber is usually part of the agitator cap; it may have a suspension spring in it. Lift off the cap and examine the snubber. If the spring is broken, or the pad is visibly worn, replace the entire snubber. Snubbers might also be found at the splash guard at the top of the tub, under the transmission, or as part of the water pump housing.

If the machine doesn't have a snubber, listen for noise at the suspension unit between the tub and the machine cabinet. The suspension unit has fins or pads that may need replacement; in some cases, the entire unit may have to be replaced. Another noise point is the basket support nut. Tighten the nut, or, if you can't tighten it, replace it.

Sudden tub stops can be caused by a broken motor belt, but they are usually due to poor tub loading. Check to see if laundry is wadded around the bottom of the tub shaft, under the basket or agitator assembly. Remove the basket or agitator to remove the laundry.

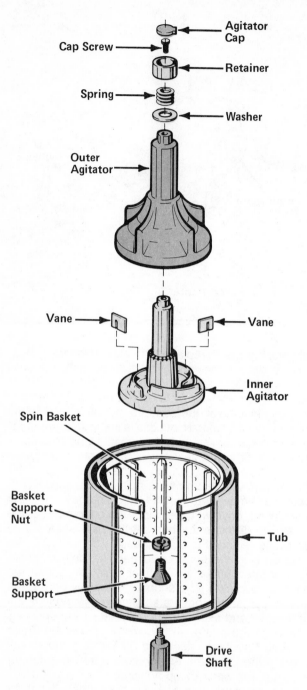

Cap Screw — Agitator Cap

Retainer

Spring

Washer

Outer Agitator

Vane — **Vane**

Inner Agitator

Spin Basket

Basket Support Nut

Tub

Basket Support

Drive Shaft

Replace a damaged agitator with a new one of the same type. Unscrew the cap on top of the agitator and pull straight up; the agitator should lift off.

Water Leaks. Water leaks in a washer are difficult to trace. The problem could be a loose connection, a broken hose, a cracked component, or a defective seal; it could also be a hole in the tub. If a hole in the tub is the problem, it's best to replace the washer.

Most leaks can be eliminated by tightening water connections and replacing deteriorated components. To stop a leak, check the lid seal, the hoses at faucet connections, the hoses at water valve connections, the drain hoses, the inlet nozzles, the splash guard, any plastic valve, the outlet hose to the drain, and the water pump. Tighten all loose connections and replace all faulty parts with new ones made for the washer.

Oil Leaks. Oil on the floor under the washer could be a sign of problems with the transmission; it could also be caused by a faulty drain plug gasket. First, check the drain plug gasket. Tip the washer over on its front, using a heavy blanket or pad to protect the washer's finish. Remove the drain plug and check the gasket; if it is worn, cracked, or no longer flexible, it should be replaced. The gasket is held in place by a screw, or is slip-fit. Remove the old gasket and replace it with a new one made to fit the washer, as detailed in the section on gaskets in "Basic Appliance Repair Principles." Put the drain plug back and stand the washer up. If this stops the oil leak, no further repairs are needed. If it doesn't, oil could be leaking from the oil pump or around the gasket under the transmission. In this case, don't try to fix the machine yourself, call a professional service person.

Water Pump. Of all washing machine parts, the water pump probably takes the most punishment, because it is constantly in use. When the pump fails, you can hear or see the trouble: a loud rumbling inside the machine, or a failure of the water to drain out of the tub. These symptoms can also be caused by kinked or crimped drain hoses, or by blocked inlet screens, so before you start work on the water pump, make sure the drain hoses are draining properly. Remove the water supply hoses from the back of the washer. With long-nosed pliers, extract the filter screens from the valve ports in the washer, or from the hoses themselves. Wash the screens thoroughly, and then replace them and reattach the hoses. If the machine still rumbles or doesn't drain, examine the pump.

To gain access to the pump, bail and sponge out any water in the machine's tub, then tip the washer over on its front, using a heavy blanket or pad to protect the washer's finish. Remove the back service panel. The pump is usually along the bottom of the machine, but with the unit tipped on its front, it's easier to remove the pump through the back than through the bottom of the washer. Locate the pump; it has two large hoses attached to it with spring or strap clips. If the clips are the spring type, pinch the ends of the clips together with pliers to release them, and slide the clips down the hoses. If the clips are the strap type, unscrew the metal collar to loosen the clamp, and disconnect the hoses by pulling them off the connections. If the hoses are kinked or crimped at these connections, straighten and reconnect them, and try the machine again to see if this kinking was causing the problem. If the machine still doesn't drain, you'll have to remove the water pump.

To remove the pump, loosen the bolt that holds the drive belt taut and move the washer motor on the bracket to loosen the belt. Move the motor out of the way and unbolt the pump; it's usually held by two or three hex-head bolts located on the bottom of the pump housing. As you loosen the last mounting bolt, support the pump with your hand. Then lift the pump out of the washer.

On some washers, the housing that covers the pump parts can be removed. If you can take the pump apart, do so, because the trouble could be lint or dirt or pieces of cloth or paper clogging the pump impeller. Clean away all debris inside the pump, and clear any debris out of the water tubes; then reassemble the pump. Hook up the pump again and test it. If cleaning the pump doesn't put it back into working order, or if the pump housing can't be removed, replace the pump with a new one made for the washer.

To install the new pump, set it into position and connect the mounting bolts to the pump housing. Move the motor back into position. Tighten the drive belt on the motor by prying it taut with a hammer handle or pry bar; it should give about ½ inch when you press on it at the center point between the two pulleys. Finally, reconnect the hoses leading to the pump.

Drive Belts and Pulleys. The drive belt (or belts) of a washing machine may become worn or damaged, causing noisy operation or stopping the washer entirely. A damaged drive belt is easy to replace. Remove the back panel of the washer to gain access to the belt.

To remove the belt, loosen the bolt on the motor bracket, and move the motor to put slack in the belt. Remove the old belt and stretch a new one into place on the pulleys. To tension the new belt, use a hammer handle or a short pry bar to push the motor into position while you tighten the bolt in the adjustable bracket. The belt should have about ½ inch deflection when you press on it at the center point, midway between the pulleys. If the belt is too loose, it will slip on the pulleys, causing the machine to malfunction. If the belt is too tight, it will wear very quickly, and will probably become so hot that it will start to smoke or smell.

Loose pulleys can also cause problems. Most pulleys are fastened to shafts with setscrews around the hub of the pulley. These screws must be tight or the pulley or belt will slip. The resultant malfunction may seem to be caused by a faulty motor, but it can be corrected by tightening the pulleys and adjusting the belt. For this reason, always check the belts and pulleys before working on the motor.

Motor. In most cases, motor malfunctions should be handled by a professional; do not try to fix the motor yourself. If the motor is a universal motor, however, you can change worn carbon brushes when sparking occurs, as detailed earlier in this chapter. You can also

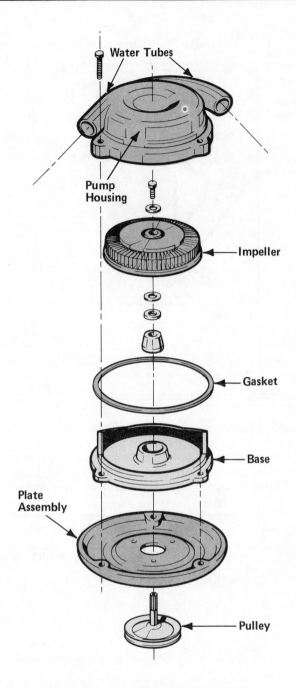

If you can, take the pump apart, and clean away all debris inside the pump. Also clear away debris from the water tubes.

save the expense of a service call by removing the motor from the washer and taking it to a professional service person, and by reinstalling the repaired or new motor. To gain access to the motor, remove the back panel of the washer. The motor is mounted on an adjustable bracket.

There is one other motor problem you can repair

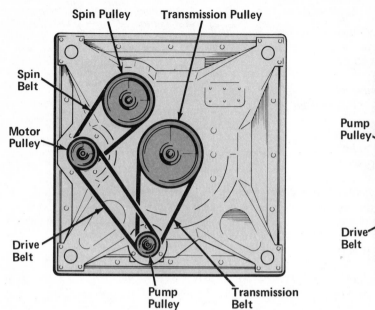

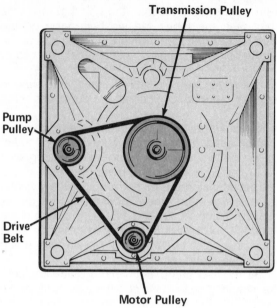

Worn or damaged drive belts can cause noisy operation or stop the washer completely. Two common belt arrangements are shown here.

yourself. Washer motors usually have an overload protector clipped to the motor. When this component fails, the motor won't work. Before you take the motor in for service, test the protector with a VOM, set to the R × 1 scale. The meter should read zero; if the needle jumps higher, the protector is faulty, and should be replaced. Pry up the protector with a screwdriver, and replace it with a new one made specifically for the motor or washer. Connect the new protector the same way the old one was connected.

Washer Troubleshooting Chart

Caution: Disconnect power and water before inspecting or repairing.

PROBLEM	POSSIBLE CAUSE	SOLUTION
Washer doesn't run	1. No power.	1. Check power cord, plug, and outlet. Check for blown fuses or tripped circuit breakers at main entrance panel; restore circuit.
	2. Motor overload or safety shutoff.	2. Press reset button on control panel or motor.
	3. Timer faulty.	3. Make sure timer is properly set. Test timers; if faulty, replace.
	4. Lid switch faulty.	4. Remove detergent buildup from orifice; make sure switch is secure and making contact. Test switch; if faulty, replace. Make sure new switch is properly aligned.
	5. Off-balance switch faulty.	5. Test switch; if faulty, replace.
	6. Water pump clogged.	6. Clean out pump, if possible; otherwise, call a professional.

Washer Troubleshooting Chart (Continued)

PROBLEM	POSSIBLE CAUSE	SOLUTION
Washer doesn't run (continued)	7. Motor binding.	7. Remove motor and take to a professional.
Fuses blow	1. Too much detergent.	1. Suds can cause problem; reduce amount of detergent used.
	2. Motor overload protector faulty.	2. Replace overload protector.
	3. Machine overloaded.	3. Reduce size of load; load properly to reduce drag on tub.
	4. Motor faulty.	4. Remove motor and take to a professional.
Tub doesn't fill	1. Supply hoses kinked or clogged.	1. Straighten hoses; clean water inlet valve screens.
	2. Water level switch faulty.	2. Remove switch and take to a professional for testing; if faulty, replace.
	3. Water inlet valve solenoids faulty.	3. Clean water inlet valves; tap solenoids lightly with screwdriver handle; if no result, replace water inlet valves.
Tub fills at wrong cycle	1. Water inlet valve solenoids faulty.	1. Clean water inlet valves; tap solenoids lightly with screwdriver handle; if no result, replace water inlet valves.
	2. Water level switch faulty.	2. Remove switch and take to a professional for testing; if faulty, replace.
	3. Pump valve stuck.	3. Remove pump and clean.
Water doesn't shut off	1. Hose to water level switch disconnected or faulty.	1. Reconnect or replace hose.
	2. Water inlet valve faulty.	2. Clean inlet valve; if problem persists, replace valve.
Tub won't empty	1. Drain hose kinked.	1. Straighten drain hose.
	2. Pump jammed or clogged.	2. Remove and clean pump; if necessary, replace.
	3. Motor belt slipping or broken.	3. Adjust or replace belt.
	4. Pump pulley loose or worn.	4. Tighten setscrews holding pulley; if necessary, replace pulley.
	5. Pump impeller faulty.	5. Replace pump.
Water too hot or too cold	1. Temperature selector switch set wrong.	1. Make sure water temperature switches on control panel are set properly.

Washer Troubleshooting Chart (Continued)

PROBLEM	POSSIBLE CAUSE	SOLUTION
Water too hot or too cold (continued)	2. Water heater temperature set wrong.	2. Check water temperature thermostat on water heater; if necessary, reset.
	3. Supply hoses reversed.	3. Switch water hoses at faucets; "hot" hose may be connected to "cold" inlet.
	4. Mixing valve faulty.	4. Check solenoid on valve; if faulty, replace valve.
	5. Temperature selector switch faulty.	5. Test switch; if faulty, replace.
	6. Timer faulty.	6. Make sure timer is properly set. Test timer; if faulty, replace.
Tub fills slowly	1. Water inlet valve screens clogged.	1. Clean water inlet valve screens.
	2. Fill spout clogged.	2. Clean fill spout.
	3. Water pressure low.	3. Call water company.
Water level low	1. Water inlet valve screens clogged.	1. Clean water inlet valve screens.
	2. Fill spout clogged.	2. Clean fill spout.
	3. Water pressure low.	3. Call water company.
High water level or overflow	1. Flow valve washer faulty or wrong size.	1. Replace flow valve washer.
	2. Water pressure too high.	2. Call water company; reduce flow by closing water faucets slightly.
	3. Water level control switch faulty.	3. Check and repair hose connected to switch. Remove switch and take to a professional for testing; if faulty, replace.
Tub spins in wash cycle	1. Timer contacts bad.	1. Test timer; if faulty, replace.
	2. Timer improperly wired.	2. Call a professional.
Oil leaks on floor	1. Drain plug faulty.	1. Replace gasket on drain plug.
	2. Support gasket faulty.	2. Call a professional.
	3. Gasket between washer housing and base faulty.	3. Call a professional.
	4. Oil pump faulty.	4. Call a professional.
	5. Vent tube leaking.	5. Solder tube shut, or call a professional.

Washer Troubleshooting Chart (Continued)

PROBLEM	POSSIBLE CAUSE	SOLUTION
Wash tangled	1. Not enough water.	1. See "Water level low."
	2. Improper loading.	2. Follow manufacturer's loading instructions.
	3. Extend washing time.	3. Follow manufacturer's control setting instructions.
	4. Agitator pulsator clearance not properly set.	4. Call a professional.
Excessive washer vibration	1. Machine not level.	1. Adjust leveling legs; check for level front to back and side to side.
	2. Tub unbalanced.	2. Follow manufacturer's loading instructions.
	3. Oversudsing.	3. Reduce amount of detergent.
	4. Tub faulty.	4. Replace tub, or replace washer.
	5. Snubber plate on water pump dirty.	5. Clean plate.
	6. Tub bolts loose.	6. Tighten nut that holds tub, replace tub, or replace washer.
	7. Cross brace damaged.	7. Call a professional.
	8. Supports loose.	8. Call a professional.
Washer rips laundry	1. Machine overloaded.	1. Follow manufacturer's loading instructions.
	2. Agitator rough or cracked.	2. Inspect agitator for rough spots and cracks; if necessary, replace.
	3. Rough spot in tub.	3. Smooth rough spot, replace tub, or replace washer.
Water leaks	1. Oversudsing.	1. Reduce amount of detergent.
	2. Fill nozzle out of alignment.	2. Align fill nozzle so it squirts into tub.
	3. Overflow nozzle out of alignment.	3. Align overflow so it squirts into drain.
	4. Fill tube faulty.	4. Replace fill tube.
	5. Lid seal faulty.	5. Replace lid seal.
	6. Hose connections loose or faulty.	6. Tighten hose connections; if hoses faulty, replace.
	7. Bolts on pump impeller loose.	7. Tighten bolts.
	8. Hole in tub.	8. Replace tub, or replace washer.
	9. Pump gasket faulty.	9. Replace gasket, if possible; otherwise, replace pump.

Water Heaters

Water heaters rarely break down, but they do require regular maintenance. Maintenance is largely a matter of cleaning dirt and dust away from the outside of the unit, and draining the tank periodically to prevent sediment buildup. This basic attention is enough to keep most water heaters running trouble-free. When repairs are necessary, it's sometimes easier to replace the entire water heater than to repair it yourself or have it repaired; the cost of a new water heater is surprisingly low, and some heaters have a warranty of up to 10 years.

The water heater consists of an insulated tank and a heat source—electric elements, or a gas or oil burner—surrounded by a cabinet. A water supply pipe carries cold water into the top of the tank, and continues into the tank as a tube called the dip tube to feed cold water in at the bottom of the tank. In some water heaters, the supply line enters the bottom of the tank directly. In both types of water heaters, heated water rises to the top of the tank, and exits via a hot-water supply line at the top of the tank. Because hot water—like hot air—rises, the water that leaves the tank to supply hot water throughout the house is always the hottest water in the tank.

All water heaters have thermostats, which are manually set to control the temperature of the water. A normal setting is between 120° and 160° F, depending on your family's hot-water needs. If your family is large, with lots of laundry, a dishwasher, and a shower/bath combination, a higher setting—160° F—is best.

Caution: Before you do any work on a water heater, turn off all power to the unit; at the main entrance panel, remove the fuse or trip the circuit breaker that controls the power to the heater. If the heater is gas-fueled, close the valve on the supply line that feeds gas to the heater. Finally, turn off the water supply to the heater.

Draining. The water heater should be drained every 30 to 60 days, year-round. If you live in a hard-water area, it's a good idea to drain the tank monthly. To drain the heater, open the drain valve on the lower side of the tank and let the water run into a bucket until it runs clear. This prevents sediment from building up in the bottom of the tank, which helps eliminate noise problems, and keeps the heater running more efficiently. When the water runs clear, close the drain valve. Finally, open the relief valve at the top of the tank to flush away accumulated sediment.

Caution: If the water heater has been in service for a long time without being drained, do not drain it. Opening the drain valve could cause leaks. If the heater has never been drained or hasn't been drained in a long time, the drain valve may be corroded; in this case, opening the valve could break it, causing a flood. Before opening the drain valve, check for corrosion. If the valve is corroded, do not open it to drain.

When the drain valve is corroded, consider replacement of the heater if repairs are necessary; draining the tank for repairs could result in a leaky drain valve. While valve replacement is relatively simple, as detailed below, replacing the valve and repairing the unit may not be worth the trouble.

Cleaning. Both the outside and the inside of the water heater must be kept clean. Vacuum the outside of the water heater to remove dirt and improve the unit's running efficiency. If the outside of the tank is very dirty, clean it with a solution of mild household detergent and water. The chimney of a gas water heater should be cleaned at least every other year. This is a messy job, but it can result in fuel savings and cut down on repairs and replacements. Electric water heaters, because they do not involve combustion, don't have chimneys, so they don't require the same overall cleaning as gas units.

To clean a gas heater chimney or vent, turn off the power and the gas to the unit, and let the heater cool. Spread newspaper to protect the floor. Open the inspection door at the bottom of the water heater and spread several layers of newspaper over the burner head. As you clean the heater, soot will fall through it onto the newspaper. Work from the top of the water heater down. The chimney of the heater is slipped together in sections; to disassemble it, separate the sections and take them down. The sections are sometimes fastened with sheet metal screws; in this case, remove the sheet metal screws for disassembly.

Start at the top of the chimney where it turns to run horizontally, and remove the sections one by one. Label each section for proper reassembly, and set each section on the newspaper. Clean the inside of each section with a wire brush and a vacuum cleaner or shop vacuum. Chimney brushes, available at home centers and some hardware stores, also work well for this job, or the sections can be cleaned with newspaper, crumpled into a solid ball and pulled through with a piece of string. At the base of the chimney, remove the draft-diverting collar around the chimney, and clean it.

At the top of the water heater, under the collar, look into the vent pipe opening exposed by the removal of the chimney. Inside the vent pipe in the tank is the flue baffle, a twisted metal strip that slows hot air rising through the pipe to transfer as much heat as possible to the water in the tank. To keep the flue baffle working properly, remove all accumulated soot from it — if there's enough room overhead, pull the baffle straight out to clean it; if there isn't, rattle it up and down to dislodge dirt. Use a wire brush and vacuum to clean all exposed baffle surfaces.

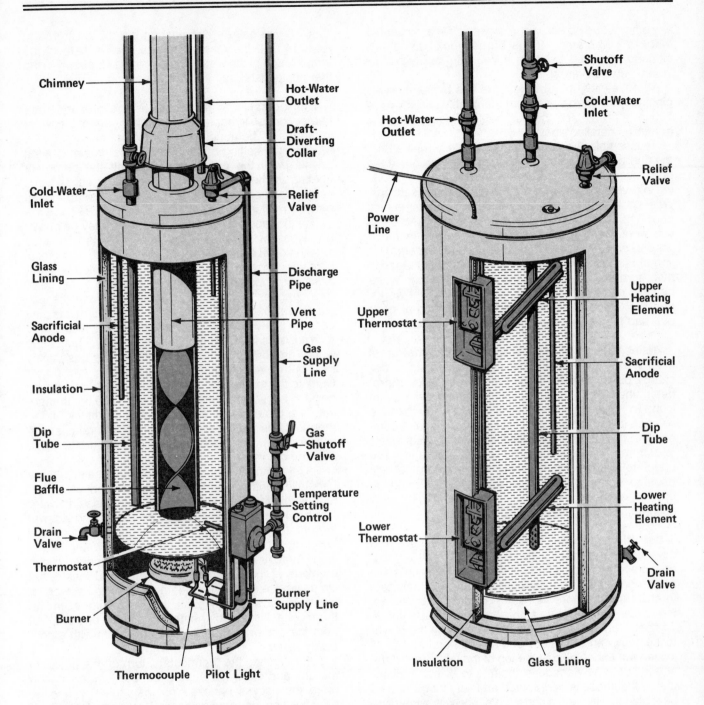

Chimney

Hot-Water Outlet

Draft-Diverting Collar

Cold-Water Inlet

Relief Valve

Glass Lining

Discharge Pipe

Sacrificial Anode

Vent Pipe

Gas Supply Line

Insulation

Dip Tube

Flue Baffle

Gas Shutoff Valve

Drain Valve

Temperature Setting Control

Thermostat

Burner

Burner Supply Line

Thermocouple   Pilot Light

Shutoff Valve

Hot-Water Outlet

Cold-Water Inlet

Power Line

Relief Valve

Upper Thermostat

Upper Heating Element

Sacrificial Anode

Dip Tube

Lower Thermostat

Lower Heating Element

Drain Valve

Insulation   Glass Lining

A gas water heater (left) consists of a tank and a gas burner inside an insulated cabinet.
Electric water heaters (right) use heating elements instead of a burner to heat water.

If you can pull the flue baffle out, remove it entirely. Then clean the vent pipe in the tank with crumpled newspaper and string, as described above. Drop the newspaper into the top of the vent pipe, and pull it through to the bottom of the water heater. Repeat, pulling the ball of newspaper up and down through the pipe, until the pipe is clean.

At the bottom of the water heater, carefully remove the protective newspaper and the dislodged soot from the burner head. Remove dirt from the burner assembly with a vacuum cleaner or a shop vacuum. Examine the burner to make sure all orifices are clear; if any opening is clogged by dirt or corrosion, reopen it with a piece of thin wire. *Caution: Do not use a toothpick or* any other wood object; wood broken off in a port could block it completely. If the burner looks extremely clogged, don't try to clean it yourself; call a professional service person.

After cleaning the chimney, the flue baffle, the vent pipe, and the burner, vacuum thoroughly to remove all debris; then replace the flue baffle. Finally, drain the heater as detailed above.

Reassemble the water heater carefully. Make sure the flue baffle is properly positioned; then replace the draft-diverting collar over the chimney opening. Working in reverse order, reassemble the chimney sections; push each section firmly into place to join it to the next one. Replace sheet metal screws section by section as you work. *Caution: Be careful to make the final joint secure, and make sure the entire chimney assembly is firm and stable.* When the chimney is firmly reassembled, turn on the gas to the unit and relight the water heater's pilot light. To make sure the pilot light works, turn the temperature dial down until the burner goes out, and then turn it up again to the proper setting.

Relief Valve. The relief valve, fitted into the top of most water heaters, lets water escape through a discharge pipe when the water pressure exceeds a predetermined limit — normally 150 pounds per square inch. To make sure the valve is working, squeeze the lever on it; this should open the discharge pipe. A combination pressure/temperature relief valve also reacts to extreme increases in water temperature; the valve opens to release steam if the temperature in the tank rises to about 210° F. The relief valve should be opened every time the tank is drained to flush away accumulated sediment.

Sacrificial Anode. Inside the heater's tank is a magnesium rod called a sacrificial anode. This component prevents corrosion of tank parts that may not have been completely corrosion-proofed by the manufacturer. In areas where the water supply is very acidic, the anode itself can be eaten away within a few years. To check for corrosion of the anode, turn off the power to the heater and let it cool. Use an open-end wrench to loosen the anode plug at the top of the tank, and lift the anode out. A new anode is about ½ to ¾ inch in diameter; if the anode is badly pitted and very thin, it should be replaced. Replace a corroded anode with a new one specifically made for the water heater; apply pipe sealant to the threads of the plug, lower the anode into place, and tighten the plug with the wrench.

Temperature Setting Control. The temperature setting control, or thermostat control, is a manual temperature control, and is present on all water heaters. The control has various numbered temperature settings on it, or is labeled "warm," "normal," and "hot," or "W," "N," and "H." The proper setting for the water heater is between 120° and 160° F, or "normal" to "hot." If you have a dishwasher, set the control to at least 140°. If the manual control does not affect the temperature of the water, the problem is probably in the thermostat itself, not in the manual control dial.

Thermostat. The thermostat is the primary water heater control; it regulates the temperature of the water in the tank. The temperature of the water rises until it reaches the setting on the manual thermostat control; at this point the thermostat shuts off the burner or heating element. If the heater won't heat up, or won't heat the water to the set temperature, the thermostat may be malfunctioning.

The thermostat of a gas water heater may be one of two types of switches. One type consists of a tube sensing device that opens and closes a set of electrical contacts. Another type consists of a gas-filled bellows, which expands and contracts in response to temperature changes; it is used to open and close the gas supply valve. In either type, the electrical contacts may become pitted and cause problems. If you suspect the thermostat is faulty, turn off the gas supply, shut off the water, and drain the tank. Disconnect the gas supply line, burner supply line, pilot supply line, and power wires to the thermostat; then remove the thermostat by backing out several retaining screws. Take the thermostat to a professional service person for testing. If the thermostat is faulty, replace it with one made specifically for the water heater; install the new one the same way the old thermostat was installed.

The thermostat of an electric water heater uses a bimetallic control to turn the heating element on and off to maintain the preset temperature. Most electric water heaters have two thermostats, an upper and a lower thermostat, which control corresponding upper and lower heating elements. If an electric water heater won't heat, first check for blown fuses or tripped circuit breakers at the main entrance panel, and restore the circuit if necessary. If the heater is receiving power, let the heater cool; then push the reset button on the thermostat. If the water heater still doesn't operate, test both the upper and the lower thermostats with a continuity tester.

Before testing the thermostats, turn off the power to the unit and the water supply. Let the tank cool; then open the access panels. You may have to pry the panels open or remove several retaining screws. If there is any insulation in the thermostat housing, pull or cut it away, but save it to replace when you replace the thermostats. If the upper thermostat is sealed and not accessible, you will have to call a professional service person to test or replace it, but if you can get to it, test it yourself.

To test the upper thermostat, hook the clip of a continuity tester to the left thermostat terminal and touch the probe to the other terminal on the left side. If the light does not glow or the tester does not buzz, the thermostat is faulty, and should be replaced. To test the lower thermostat, remove the housing or service panel from the thermostat. Hook the clip of the continuity tester to the left terminal and touch the probe to the other terminal. If the light does not glow or the tester does not buzz, replace the thermostat. To replace either of the two thermostats, use a new thermostat made specifically for the water heater. Install the new thermostat the way the old one was installed.

On many electric heaters, a safety interlock device—usually located near the top of the tank and often

Gas Water Heater Troubleshooting Chart

Caution: Disconnect power and fuel before inspecting or repairing.

PROBLEM	POSSIBLE CAUSE	SOLUTION
No hot water	1. No power.	1. Check for blown fuses or tripped circuit breakers at main entrance panel; restore circuit.
	2. Pilot light out.	2. Relight pilot.
	3. No gas.	3. Make sure gas valve is open; if no result, call gas company.
	4. Temperature control set wrong.	4. Make sure temperature is set between 120° and 160° F.
	5. Thermostat faulty.	5. Remove thermostat and take to professional; if faulty, replace.
Pilot won't stay lit	1. Thermocouple faulty.	1. Replace thermocouple.
	2. Burner dirty.	2. Call a professional.
	3. Gas supply valve not open.	3. Open gas supply valve fully.
	4. Little or no gas.	4. Call gas company.
Water not hot enough	1. Temperature control set too low.	1. Set temperature between 120° and 160° F.
	2. Hot-water faucets dripping.	2. Repair leaky faucets throughout house.
	3. Pipes losing heat.	3. Insulate hot-water pipes.
	4. Thermostat faulty.	4. Remove thermostat and take to professional; if faulty, replace.
	5. Burner dirty.	5. Call a professional.
	6. Sediment in tank.	6. If unit new, drain on schedule; if old, call a professional.
	7. Tank too small.	7. Replace with larger tank.
Water too hot	1. Temperature control set too high.	1. Set temperature between 120° and 160° F.
	2. Thermostat faulty.	2. Remove thermostat and take to professional; if faulty, replace.
	3. Vent blocked.	3. Check for outward heat draft; if no draft, call a professional.
	4. Hot-water faucets dripping.	4. Repair leaky faucets throughout house.
Tank leaks	1. Rust in tank.	1. Have unit replaced.
Noisy operation	1. Sediment in tank.	1. Drain tank.
	2. Draft on burner.	2. Some burner noise is normal.

mounted above the top thermostat — turns off the power to both elements if the water heater overheats. To reset a tripped safety interlock, turn off the power to the heater, remove the front access panel, and push the reset button. If the device kicks out a second time, the elements could be faulty. In this case, follow the procedures below to solve the problem. Use a thermometer at a nearby faucet to determine whether the water is actually overheating.

Electric Heating Elements. When electricity is the power source for a water heater, the tank contains upper and lower heating elements, corresponding to the upper and lower thermostats, to provide the heat. The heating elements are located in the tank, directly behind and slightly below the thermostat control. The elements are bolted onto a flange mounted to the outside of the tank; a gasket seal protects them against water leakage. If the upper thermostat is sealed and inaccessible, the upper heating element will also not be accessible. Call a professional service person to test or replace this sealed element.

When you suspect a faulty heating element, test it with a continuity tester. Turn off the power to the heater and the water supply, and let the heater cool. Hook the clip of the continuity tester to one terminal of the element and touch the probe to any retaining bolt inside the element housing. If the tester lights or buzzes, the element is faulty, and should be replaced. Replace the element with a new one of the same type.

To replace the element, leave the power and the water off, and drain the water from the tank. Disconnect the power wires to the element, and remove the retaining screws that hold the element to the heater housing. Then pull the element out of the tank. After you remove the element you may discover that it's covered with mineral deposits. In this case, you may be able to clean the element; soak it in vinegar and brush it clean, and reinstall it to see if it works. This procedure isn't always successful, but it's worth trying before you buy a new element.

Replace the faulty element with a new one of exactly the same type; take the element to an appliance parts store to make sure you get the right type. Also buy a new gasket to seal the element where it's mounted to the tank. Install the new element and connect it the same way the old one was connected. Using the new gasket, bolt the element into place on the tank flange. Then, with the new element in place, fill the tank with water. Finally, turn on the power and make the necessary temperature control settings.

Gas Burners. A professional service person should service the burner on a gas water heater; schedule this service annually. If the burner of a gas water heater is not operating properly, do not try to clean it or make any repairs — the procedures involved could be hazardous, and special equipment is required. Only a professional service person should repair, clean, or replace the gas burner.

Pilot Light. Gas water heaters have a pilot light, located next to the burner. The pilot operates like the pilot light on a gas range, and is controlled by the combination temperature control near the bottom of the heater.

If the pilot light goes out, relight it. Turn the gas valve to the "pilot" setting on the control box. Press the reset button next to the gas valve, and hold the button down while holding a lighted match to the pilot orifice. Keep the button depressed until the flame is burning steadily. On most gas heaters, relighting instructions are embossed on a metal tag just above the combination control, or fastened to the top of the heater. Because the reset button shuts off the gas supply to the burner, there is no danger when lighting the pilot. However, use caution when relighting the pilot light.

If there is an adjustment screw—it will be labeled—on or near the gas valve, you can adjust the height of the pilot light by turning the screw. Turn the screw slightly counterclockwise to open the valve, slightly clockwise to close it. The pilot flame should be about one inch high; it should just touch the thermocouple.

Thermocouple. The thermocouple in a gas water heater operates as a safety device, to turn the gas supply off when the pilot light goes out. It consists of a heat sensor connected to a solenoid; when the sensor is not heated by the pilot flame, the solenoid closes the gas supply line. When the thermocouple fails, the pilot light won't stay lighted; the thermocouple may be burned out or broken. A faulty thermocouple should be replaced.

To replace a thermocouple, unscrew the copper lead and the connection nut inside the threaded connection to the gas line. Under the mounting bracket at the thermocouple tube, unscrew the bracket nut that holds the tube in place. Insert a new thermocouple into the hole in the bracket, steel tube up and copper lead down. Under the bracket, screw the bracket nut over the tube. Push the connection nut to the threaded connection where the copper lead connects to the gas line; make sure the connection is clean and dry. Screw the nut tightly into place, but do not overtighten it. Both the bracket nut and the connection nut should be only a little tighter than hand-tightened.

Drain Leaks. All water heaters have a drain valve, similar to a faucet. If this valve is leaking, turn off the water and drain the tank. Then disassemble the faucet by removing the handle, cap, and valve stem. At the bottom of the stem is a washer. Replace this washer with a new one of the same type and size, and reassemble the faucet. If the faucet continues to leak, replace the faucet with a new one of the same type and size. The faucet is connected to a threaded pipe; unscrew the faucet with a pipe wrench to remove it. Coat the threads of the new faucet with pipe joint compound or wrap the threads with plumbers' joint tape; then insert the faucet into the threaded pipe and turn it tightly in with a pipe wrench. Turn on the water supply, and test for leaks. If the joint leaks, tighten the joint.

Tank Leaks. When the tank of a water heater springs a leak, the entire water heater should be replaced; it doesn't pay to try to repair the tank. Buy a new tank of the same size and the same fuel type, and call a professional service person to handle the replacement.

Electric Water Heater Troubleshooting Chart

Caution: Disconnect power before inspecting or repairing.

PROBLEM	POSSIBLE CAUSE	SOLUTION
No hot water	1. No power.	1. Check for blown fuses or tripped circuit breakers at main entrance panel; restore circuit.
	2. Safety interlock tripped.	2. Press reset button.
	3. Temperature control set wrong.	3. Make sure temperature is set between 120° and 160° F.
	4. Upper thermostat faulty.	4. If possible, remove and test thermostat; if faulty, replace. Or call a professional.
	5. Lower thermostat faulty.	5. Test thermostat; if faulty, replace.
	6. Upper heating element faulty.	6. If possible, remove and test element; if faulty, replace. Or call a professional.
	7. Lower heating element faulty.	7. Test element; if faulty, replace.
Water not hot enough	1. Temperature control set too low.	1. Set temperature between 120° and 160° F.
	2. Hot-water faucets dripping.	2. Repair leaky faucets throughout house.
	3. Pipes losing heat.	3. Insulate hot-water pipes.
	4. Thermostat faulty.	4. If possible, remove and test thermostat; if faulty, replace. Or call a professional.
	5. Sediment in tank.	5. If unit new, drain on schedule; if old, call a professional.
	6. Tank too small.	6. Replace with larger tank.
Water too hot	1. Temperature control set too high.	1. Set temperature between 120° and 160° F.
	2. Thermostat faulty.	2. If possible, remove and test thermostat; if faulty, replace. Or call a professional.
	3. Hot-water faucets dripping.	3. Repair leaky faucets throughout house.
Tank leaks	1. Rust in tank.	1. Have unit replaced.
Noisy operation	1. Sediment in tank.	1. Drain tank.

Small Appliances

Small appliances are the archetypal convenience tools. They do all the little chores of housekeeping and some of the big ones too, from opening cans to cleaning floors. They make cooking easier. They keep us comfortable. They've become indispensable as grooming tools. They do all of these things so efficiently that the "convenience" they provide has become a necessity— and so reliably that we take it for granted that they'll always work right.

When a small appliance does fail, we're usually at a loss. Is it repairable, or is it completely dead? Is it worth the price of a professional opinion to find out? In fact, it may not be worth fixing a very small appliance; many appliances are so inexpensive that repairs—especially by a professional service person—may end up costing more than a brand-new appliance. Consider this factor before you repair any small appliance—or, if you can't fix it yourself, before taking it to a professional service person. Ask for an estimate before going ahead with any professional repairs, you could be money ahead buying a new appliance.

Although small appliances are not always worth fixing, in many cases it's well worth your time to make the repairs. The troubleshooting charts in this section will help you spot the problem and make the fix/no-fix decision. And once you've decided the job is worth doing, the repair procedures detailed below will help you get your appliances back in working order, in no time.

Most small appliances of the same type operate on the same basic principles, so repairs to most models are similar or identical, no matter what brand is involved. Although different makes of appliances generally operate alike, they don't always conform to the same design; major brand-name appliances may look quite different. To make it even more complicated, the various manufacturers add different features to their products to help generate more sales. Because of these differences among brand-name small appliances, you should use the repair and replacement techniques in this chapter as general guidelines, not as absolute standards for specific models.

Because small appliance operation does follow the same principles, it's easy to be tempted into buying repair parts that look alike or "fit all." This is not a good idea — replacement parts must match the make and model of the appliance being repaired. Many appliances have a tag with the model number and other identifying information, attached to the back or the bottom of the appliance; others have this information stamped into the appliance housing. If you can't find this information, take the part or the whole appliance to an appliance parts store or appliance repair outlet that sells replacement parts. The dealer should be able to identify the part for you and provide the proper replacement. Parts can also be ordered directly from the manufacturer.

There is one other big consideration in repairing small appliances. If the parts of the appliance are held together with screws, or friction-fit with plugs, you'll probably be able to repair it with no problem. If the parts are riveted or welded together, this is not true; you could do more harm than good by trying to disassemble it. Take this type of appliance — if it's worth fixing — to a professional service person.

Blenders

Blenders, like mixers, have become essential kitchen tools, for chopping, blending, pureeing, and liquefying foods. A blender consists of a glass or plastic container on a base that houses a universal motor, and a chopper blade assembly inside the container, powered by the motor in the base. Most blender problems involve the blades and shaft that make up the chopper assembly.

Caution: Before doing any work on a blender, make sure it is unplugged.

Disassembly. To work on a blender, you must disassemble the chopper assembly and open the base to get at the motor. The container may be in one piece, with the cutter blades sealed in the bottom of the unit. To release the blades, remove the container from the base and loosen the coupling nut at the bottom of the container. Using a cloth to protect your fingers, hold the blades inside the container and turn the coupler clockwise to loosen it; then remove the blades. If the parts don't move, turn the coupler counterclockwise to loosen it; some couplers come off this way. Until you're sure which way to turn the coupler to remove it, don't use a lot of force; you could break it.

To get at the motor, detach the coupler on the top of the base. If the motor shaft is threaded, use a screwdriver to hold the shaft and keep it from rotating; turn the coupler clockwise to remove it. On some units the coupler turns counterclockwise for removal. If the coupling consists of a metal stud that slips into the bottom of the container, slip a nail through a ventilating hole on the bottom of the base, and engage the blades of the fan with the nail to keep the shaft from rotating. Then loosen the stud with an adjustable wrench by turning it either clockwise or counterclockwise.

Cleaning. The fan and chopper blade assembly of a blender should be cleaned periodically to keep the blender working efficiently. To clean the blades, remove the coupling from the container, and take out the blades, shaft, washers, bearing housing, and nuts that make up the chopper assembly. Lay out the parts in order as you disassemble the blender, and make a diagram as you work so you'll be able to reassemble the chopper correctly. Clean the parts in a solution of water and mild household detergent, and dry them thoroughly. Examine the chopper blades and the bearings carefully; they're subject to considerable wear and tear. If they look damaged, replace them with new parts made to fit the blender.

Dirt on the fan blades can cause noise. To solve this problem, remove the bottom of the base or the switch plate; use a solution of water and mild household detergent to clean the blades. Clean as much of the motor as you can reach, and also wipe the housing clean. Remove the coupler to get into the top of the base to clean the remaining parts of the motor. Be careful not to get any wires wet. After cleaning, wipe the parts dry. Let the blender air-dry thoroughly before reassembling it.

Noisy Operation. If the blender is very noisy, the problem is most likely with either the coupling or the fan. The top coupling is the bottom part of the chopper shaft assembly; the bottom coupling is at the top of the base where the container attaches to the motor. If either coupling looks worn, replace it with a new one made for the blender; install the new one the same way the old one was installed.

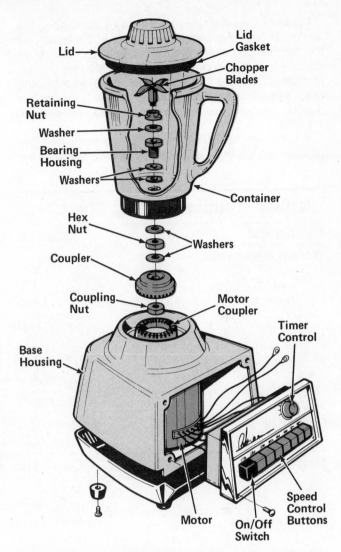

A blender has a chopper blade assembly powered by a universal motor. The motor is controlled by a switch with multiple settings.

Unusual or very loud noises are usually caused by a bent or broken fan blade. To solve this problem, open the base of the unit and clean and inspect the fan blades. If the blades are bent slightly, straighten them with pliers; if you can't straighten them, replace the entire fan blade assembly. To remove the fan blade assembly, loosen the retaining nut that holds it on the motor shaft; or, if the blade assembly is friction-fit, pull it off. Replace the fan blade assembly with a new one made for the blender; install the new assembly the same way the old one was installed.

Noise can also be caused by loose or broken chopper blades. Examine the blade assembly. If the blades are loose, tighten them; if they are broken, remove them, as detailed above, and replace them with new blades made for the blender.

Leaks. Leaks are usually caused by damage to the container or to the compression seal at the bottom of the blender container. If the container is cracked, replace it with a new one made for the blender. Plastic blender containers can sometimes develop a hairline crack which can cause leaking; look closely to spot tiny cracks. If cracks are the source of leaks, replace the container.

If there are no visible cracks in the container, the problem is probably the compression seal. Remove the chopper assembly, as detailed above, and examine the seal. If the seal is worn, split, or hard, replace it with a new seal made to fit the blender.

Leaks around the lid of the blender container are usually caused by a worn lid gasket. If this is the problem, it's best to replace the entire lid; buy a new lid made for the blender.

Switches. The motor is controlled by a switch with multiple settings, in the base of the unit. If the blender

Blender Troubleshooting Chart

Caution: Disconnect power before inspecting or repairing.

PROBLEM	POSSIBLE CAUSE	SOLUTION
Blender doesn't run	1. No power.	1. Check power cord, plug, and outlet. Check for blown fuse or tripped circuit breaker at main entrance panel; restore circuit.
	2. Switch faulty.	2. Replace switch, or take to a professional.
	3. Carbon brushes worn.	3. Check brushes; if worn, replace.
	4. Short circuit in electrical system.	4. Take to a professional.
	5. Motor faulty.	5. Take to a professional.
Blender shocks	1. Power cord faulty.	1. Test cord; if faulty, replace.
	2. Short circuit in electrical system.	2. Take to a professional.
Motor sparks	1. Carbon brushes worn.	1. Check brushes; if worn, replace.
	2. Motor faulty.	2. Take to a professional.
Motor runs slow	1. Blender container overloaded.	1. Reduce load, or add more liquid to container.
	2. Carbon brushes worn.	2. Check brushes; if worn, replace.
Motor runs but blades don't turn	1. Container not seated properly.	1. Mount container so that coupler on container meshes with coupler on base.
	2. Coupling worn or dirty.	2. Check couplers; if dirty or worn, replace.
	3. Chopper assembly dirty.	3. Clean chopper assembly.
	4. Chopper blades bent or worn.	4. Replace chopper blades.
Noisy operation	1. Chopper blades obstructed.	1. Remove obstruction from chopper.
	2. Chopper blades bent or worn.	2. Replace chopper blades.
	3. Fan blades bent.	3. Straighten blades, or replace fan blade assembly.
	4. Coupling worn.	4. Check top and bottom couplers; if worn, replace.
	5. Motor faulty.	5. Take to a professional.

has multiple switches and/or push buttons, or the switch is controlled by solid-state rectifiers behind each speed setting, don't try to fix it yourself; take the blender to an appliance repair outlet.

Single-speed switches can be replaced when they malfunction. If the blender won't run, and it is receiving power, the switch could be faulty. Open the base of the unit at the top or bottom or the switch plate, as above, and test the switch with a VOM, set to the R × 1 scale; the meter should read zero. If the switch is faulty, replace it with a new one made for the blender. Disconnect the retaining screws to remove the old switch from the mounting plate; set the new switch in the same position, connect it the same way the old one was connected, and replace the screws.

Timer. Some blenders have a timer, with a timer control located on the control panel. If the timer doesn't work, replace it with a new one made for the blender; do not try to repair it. The timer is positioned directly behind the timer control knob; to reach the timer, remove the knob. If it is friction-fit on the timer shaft, just pull it off; if it's held in place by a setscrew, back out the screw to remove the knob. Then remove the escutcheon plate that covers the switches. If there are many wires connected to the timer, and it is used to control a variety of settings, don't try to replace the timer yourself; take the blender to an appliance repair outlet. If the timer is a simple unit, however, you should be able to replace it. Remove it from its mounting bracket, and tag the connecting wires so you'll be able to replace them properly on the new timer. Set the new timer into place, connect the wires, and attach the timer to the bracket the same way the old one was attached.

Motor. If the switch has been replaced and the motor still doesn't run, or if it runs erratically, makes noise, smells, or sparks, the motor's carbon brushes are probably worn. Replace them with new carbon brushes made for the blender, as detailed in the section on motor repairs in "Basic Appliance Repair Principles." If the motor still doesn't run, or if there are more serious motor problems, such as loose armature windings or shocking, take the blender to an appliance repair outlet.

Can Openers

Electric can openers are simple mechanical devices that consist of a cutting wheel, a lever-operated switch that activates the wheel, and a motor that drives the cutting wheel. Some can openers also include a knife sharpener, driven by the same motor. The most com-

mon problems with can openers involve the cutting blade, which can quickly get dirty or dull. In most cases, these problems are easy to solve.

Caution: Before doing any work on an electric can opener, make sure it is unplugged.

Cutting Wheel. If the can opener works unevenly or if the can rotates on the opener without being cut, the problem is most likely with the cutting wheel or the spring-loaded screw through its center that maintains cutting tension. If this screw is loose, the can will rotate without being cut; tighten the screw to solve this problem. If the cutting wheel is dirty, the dirt could be keeping the wheel from turning or from cutting evenly; clean the wheel to eliminate the problem. To clean the cutting wheel, remove the spring-loaded screw through its center and remove the cutting wheel. On some units, a second screw to the left of the tension screw must also be removed. Clean the cutting wheel in a solution of water and mild household detergent, and dry it thoroughly.

If the cutting wheel is dull, replace it with a new one made for the can opener. If replacement is not convenient, or if a new part has to be ordered, you can sharpen the wheel for temporary use by stroking the cutting edge on a whetstone. Press the cutting wheel on the whetstone with your thumb and rotate the wheel slowly; try to rotate the wheel around its cutting edge. Hone the wheel evenly, with no hollow spots; then mount the wheel. Replace the cutting wheel with a new one as soon as possible.

Cutting Wheel Lever. The cutting wheel lever operates the switch; when the lever is pressed down, the switch button is depressed, activating the switch. If the can opener doesn't work, check the lever; if it's bent or broken, it might not be contacting the switch. If the lever is damaged, replace it with a new one made for the can opener. To remove the lever, remove the screw inside the opener housing that holds it. Install the new lever the same way the old one was installed.

Gears and Drive Wheel. If the opener growls, skips, or slides, the gear wheels inside the housing are malfunctioning. The most likely cause is worn or broken teeth along the rim of the gears. To reach the gears, open the can opener's housing. The gears may be screwed to their shafts or may be friction-fit; pull out or unscrew the spur gear and use a long-nosed pliers to pull off the drive wheel. On some units the drive wheel is held by a screw through the front of the unit; pull out or unscrew the idler gear. Clean the gears with a solution of water and mild household detergent, and dry them thoroughly. Then lubricate the gears with heat-resistant oil. If any of the gears is worn or broken, replace the entire gear assembly with a new one made for the can opener. Clean and lubricate the gears annually to keep the can opener working well.

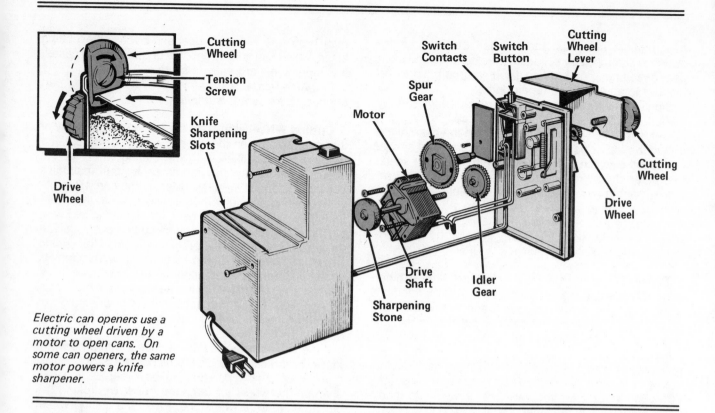

Cutting Wheel

Tension Screw

Knife Sharpening Slots

Drive Wheel

Switch Contacts

Switch Button

Cutting Wheel Lever

Spur Gear

Motor

Cutting Wheel

Drive Wheel

Drive Shaft

Idler Gear

Sharpening Stone

Electric can openers use a cutting wheel driven by a motor to open cans. On some can openers, the same motor powers a knife sharpener.

Can Opener Troubleshooting Chart

Caution: Disconnect power before inspecting or repairing.

PROBLEM	POSSIBLE CAUSE	SOLUTION
Opener doesn't run	1. No power.	1. Check power cord, plug, and outlet. Check for blown fuse or tripped circuit breaker at main entrance panel; restore circuit.
	2. Switch faulty.	2. Clean or replace switch.
	3. Gears broken.	3. Replace gears.
	4. Carbon brushes worn (universal motor).	4. Check brushes; if worn, replace.
	5. Motor faulty.	5. Take to a professional, or replace can opener.
Opener shocks	1. Power cord faulty.	1. Test cord; if faulty, replace.
	2. Short circuit in electrical system.	2. Take to a professional, or replace can opener.
Opener sparks	1. Carbon brushes worn (universal motor).	1. Check brushes; if worn, replace.
	2. Motor faulty.	2. Replace can opener.
Motor runs continuously	1. Switch faulty.	1. Replace switch.
Motor runs, but cutting wheel doesn't turn	1. Cutting wheel dirty.	1. Clean cutting wheel assembly.
	2. Cutting wheel dull.	2. Replace cutting wheel.
	3. Gears worn or damaged.	3. Replace gears.

Can Opener Troubleshooting Chart (Continued)

PROBLEM	POSSIBLE CAUSE	SOLUTION
Motor speed uneven	1. Carbon brushes worn (universal motor). 2. Speed governor faulty.	1. Check brushes; if worn, replace. 2. Take to a professional, or replace can opener.
Cutter doesn't cut into can	1. Operating lever faulty. 2. Cutting wheel dull.	1. Replace operating lever. 2. Replace cutting wheel.
Cutter doesn't completely open	1. Cutting wheel dirty. 2. Cutting wheel dull. 3. Drive wheel faulty.	1. Clean cutting wheel assembly. 2. Replace cutting wheel. 3. Replace drive wheel.

Knife Sharpener. Some can openers also have knife sharpeners. Problems with this unit are usually caused by a worn or uneven sharpening stone. Open the housing to check the sharpening stone. The stone is held to the motor's drive shaft with a screw, or is friction-fit on the shaft. If the stone is worn or uneven, replace it with a new one made to fit the opener. Attach the new stone the same way the old one was attached.

Metal filings left in the unit as a by-product of the sharpening process can also cause a problem; the filings are drawn by the magnetic force of the motor, and can cause a short circuit or damage the motor bearing. If the can opener has a knife sharpener, you should remove these filings every few months—more often if the sharpener is used frequently. Make sure there are no loose parts in the area of the motor; then remove the filings with a vacuum cleaner. If there is a heavy accumulation of filings, remove the motor by backing out the screws that hold it to the housing, and vacuum the filings from the gears and bearing. Then replace the motor.

Switch. The switch on a can opener is located directly under the cutting wheel lever. When the lever is pressed down, the switch button is depressed and the switch is activated. To clean or replace the switch, open the housing.

If the contacts of the switch are dirty, clean them, using a fine emery board to remove grease and other debris from the contact points. Turn the switch on and look at the two metal contact points under the switch button; they should touch when the button is pressed and separate when the button is released. If the points don't touch, bend them together with a long-nosed pliers. If the points are burned or pitted, replace the switch with a new one made for the can opener. The switch is held by a metal housing bracket; remove the

screws holding the switch to the bracket and take out the old switch. Connect the new switch the same way the old one was connected, and replace the housing bracket.

Motor. Most can openers are powered by a shaded-pole motor. If a can opener with this type of motor doesn't run, or if it runs erratically, makes noise, smells, or sparks, buy a new can opener; repair or replacement of the shaded-pole motor would cost more than a new opener. If the can opener has a universal motor, these problems may be caused by worn carbon brushes. Check the brushes; if they are worn, replace them with new carbon brushes made for the can opener, as detailed in the section on motor repairs in "Basic Appliance Repair Principles." If there are more serious problems in a universal motor, such as a faulty armature winding or shocking, take the can opener to an appliance repair outlet.

Electric Knives

There are two types of electric knives, operating from batteries and from regular AC current. The operating mechanics of both types are almost identical. An electric knife has two serrated blades that move back and forth, parallel to each other, at high speed. The blades are driven by a small universal or direct-current motor; the motor is specially geared to the speed needed to operate the parallel blades. Most malfunctions are caused by dull blades, or by problems in the worm gear or the retaining assembly.

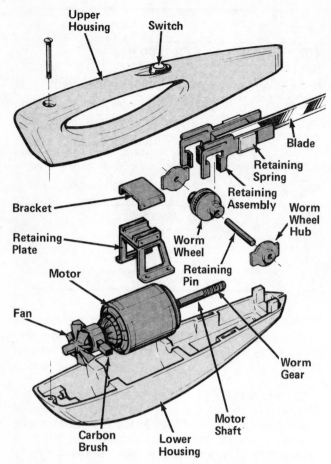

An electric knife has two serrated blades that move back and forth at high speed. Knives are powered by either AC current or by batteries.

Caution: *Before doing any work on an electric knife, make sure it is unplugged, or remove the batteries that power it.*

Cleaning and Lubrication. Electric knives accumulate a lot of grease and food debris. To keep them operating efficiently, disassemble the knife housing once a year—more often if the knife is used frequently—and clean the gear assembly. Clean the working parts carefully and thoroughly with a soft cloth; a cloth stretched over the point of a pencil makes a good tool. Wipe the outside of the motor clean with a damp cloth. Then lubricate the gear assembly with silicone gear grease.

Batteries. Cordless electric knives operate on batteries, and lack of power is often caused by dead or failing batteries. Before you make any repairs, replace the batteries and try the knife again. Knife batteries are usually nickel-cadmium cells which can be charged with a transformer supplied with the knife. If the bat-

teries will not hold a charge, replace them with new ones of the same type. Flashlight-type dry cells are not suitable for use in an electric knife; do not replace faulty batteries with this type of dry cell battery.

If the batteries of an electric knife will not charge, the transformer of the charging assembly may be faulty. Take the knife to an appliance repair outlet; repair services will usually check the transformer for no fee. If the transformer is faulty, replace it with a new one made for the electric knife. Install the new transformer the same way the old one was installed.

Blades. If the knife won't cut, or cuts slowly, the blades may be dull. In this case, replace the blades with new ones made for the knife; the old blades cannot be sharpened. Replace both blades.

Gears. Problems often occur when the worm gear at the end of the motor shaft or the worm wheel that meshes with the worm gear becomes worn. Examine the gear and the wheel. If the teeth on the worm gear are damaged or worn, replace the gear with a new one made for the knife. The worm gear fits onto the motor shaft, and may be held by a setscrew or may be friction-fit; remove the setscrew and pull off the gear, or simply pull off the gear. Install the new gear the same way the old one was installed. The worm wheel in an electric knife is usually made of plastic, and is especially prone to wear. If the teeth of the wheel are worn, replace the wheel with a new one made for the knife. To remove the worm wheel, pull out the pin at its hub that holds it in place. Check the pin for cracks. If the pin is cracked or damaged, replace the entire worm wheel assembly; do not try to mend it with a metal adhesive or filler. Install the new worm wheel or assembly the same way the old one was installed.

Retaining Assembly. The retaining assembly that holds the knife blades in place frequently wears out before the blades do. The assembly is located in the knife housing near the front end. On both sides of the assembly there is a retaining spring that secures the knife blades; if a blade won't lock into the unit, the spring is probably broken. Remove the screws holding the retaining assembly together and remove the broken spring. Replace it with a new one made to fit the knife. If the retaining assembly is cracked, replace the entire assembly with a new one made for the knife. Remove the bracket and retaining plate that cover the gear assembly to remove the retaining assembly; install the new assembly the same way the old one was installed. If the retaining assembly is held together with rivets, take the knife to an appliance repair outlet.

Switch. The control switch on an electric knife is a simple spring-loaded push button or slide on/off switch that must be held in place to keep the circuit closed. The switch assembly is located directly under the push

Electric Knife Troubleshooting Chart

Caution: *Disconnect power before inspecting or repairing.*

PROBLEM	POSSIBLE CAUSE	SOLUTION
Knife doesn't run	1. No power.	1. Check power cord, plug, and outlet. Check for blown fuse or tripped circuit breaker at main entrance panel; restore circuit.
	2. Batteries dead (battery-operated units).	2. Recharge or replace batteries.
	3. Carbon brushes worn.	3. Check brushes; if worn, replace.
	4. Switch contacts dirty.	4. Clean switch contacts.
	5. Switch faulty.	5. Test switch; if faulty, replace.
	6. Gears worn or damaged.	6. Replace gears.
	7. Speed governor faulty.	7. Take to a professional.
Knife shocks	1. Power cord faulty.	1. Test cord; if faulty, replace.
	2. Short circuit in electrical system.	2. Take to a professional.
Knife sparks	1. Carbon brushes worn.	1. Check brushes; if worn, replace.
	2. Motor faulty.	2. Take to a professional, or replace knife.
Motor runs continuously	1. Switch faulty.	1. Replace switch.
Blades don't cut	1. Blades dirty.	1. Clean blades.
	2. Blades dull.	2. Replace blades.
	3. Gears worn or damaged.	3. Replace gears.
Blades cut too slowly	1. Blades not seated properly.	1. Reseat blades so they are firmly held in retaining assembly.
	2. Blades dirty.	2. Clean blades.
	3. Blades dull.	3. Replace blades.
	4. Carbon brushes worn.	4. Check brushes; if worn, replace.
	5. Gears dirty; gears need lubrication.	5. Clean and lubricate gears.
	6. Gears worn or damaged.	6. Replace gears.

button or slide. If the switch doesn't work, open the knife and unscrew the switch from the housing. Remove dirt and grease from the switch contacts by rubbing them gently with a fine emery board, then wiping them with a soft cloth. Try the switch again. If it still doesn't work, disconnect the lead wires, which are attached with screws or friction-fit connectors. If the connectors are friction-fit, use a long-nosed pliers to grip them; don't use your fingers — you could break the wires. Test the switch with a VOM, set to the R × 1 scale; the meter should read zero. If the switch is faulty, replace it with a new one made for the knife. Connect the new switch the same way the old one was connected; then screw the switch into the housing.

Motor. If the switch has been repaired and the motor still doesn't run, or if it runs erratically, makes noise, smells, or sparks, the motor's carbon brushes are probably worn. Replace them with new carbon brushes made for the knife, as detailed in the section on motor repairs in "Basic Appliance Repair Principles." If the motor still doesn't run, or if there are more serious motor problems, such as a loose armature winding or shocking, take the knife to an appliance repair outlet.

Hair Dryers

A hair dryer has three main parts: a motor, a heating element, and a fan. When the hair dryer is turned on, the heating element gets hot and the fan blows air heated by the element out through a grille. The switch that operates the hair dryer has one or more settings. Some hair dryers have several switches, one controlling the motor and one or two controlling the heating elements. Many hair dryers are contained in a sealed plastic housing; this housing cannot be disassembled for repairs. If this type of hair dryer malfunctions, take it to an appliance repair outlet. Get a repair cost estimate before authorizing any repairs; frequently you can re-

place the dryer with a new one for less than the repairs would cost.

Caution: Before doing any work on a hair dryer, make sure it is unplugged.

Cleaning and Lubrication. The internal components of a hair dryer collect a lot of debris; while the hair dryer is turned on, dust and hairs get sucked into the air intake. Disassemble the housing and component parts periodically, and check the terminals inside the unit. If the terminals are burned, dirty, or corroded, clean them with fine steel wool and a soft cloth. Remove hair and debris from all parts. Clean the motor shaft and the bearings the fan turns on, and lubricate these parts with light household oil — sewing machine oil works well.

When you clean the hair dryer, check the on/off switch and, if the dryer has them, the switches controlling the heating elements. Clean and tighten the switch terminals. If the switch is clogged with dirt, disconnect the lead wires to it and lift the switch out. Spray the terminals and the switch with electrical contact cleaner, available at appliance repair and electrical supply outlets. Flip the switch back and forth several times to work the cleaner into the moving parts, and wipe it clean with a soft cloth; then reinstall it.

Overheating. Because the heat produced by the elements is so intense, hair dryers have an overload protector, which turns the heating elements off when too high a temperature is reached. If the dryer turns off while it's being used, disconnect it from the power source and let it cool for 30 minutes or longer; then try the hair dryer again. If it works, the problem was simply overheating; the heat overload protector has tripped and, as the dryer cooled, reset itself. If the dryer doesn't work after cooling for 30 minutes, the overload protector may be faulty. Unplug the hair dryer and open the housing. The overload protector—in most cases a thermodisc thermostat — is usually located on the heating element housing. Look for a concave or convex piece of bimetal about an inch in diameter. To determine whether the overload protector is faulty, test it with a VOM, set to the R × 1 scale; the meter should read zero. If the overload protector is faulty, replace it with a new one made for the hair dryer. Remove the old protector, and connect the new protector the same way the old one was connected.

Heating Elements. Some hair dryers have one heating element; some have two elements. If the hair dryer turns off while it's being used, and the overload protector is not faulty, the problem is usually a faulty heating element. Open the hair dryer and examine the element. If the element is broken, stretched, or sagging, it should be replaced. Replace it with a new element made for the hair dryer. Loosen the screws that hold the old element in position, disconnect the electri-

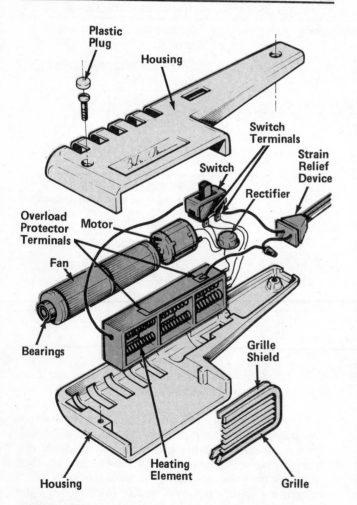

A hair dryer consists of a motor, heating elements, and a fan. Multiple switches usually control the heating elements.

cal leads, and remove the element from the dryer housing. Connect the new element the same way the old one was connected. If the old element cannot be unscrewed for replacement, take the hair dryer to an appliance repair outlet, or, if the dryer is an inexpensive one, replace the dryer.

Switches. Most hair dryers have an on/off switch that controls the motor and one or two additional switches—if there are two heating elements there will probably be two switches—that regulate the settings of the heating elements. These switches are usually wired in series; if the motor doesn't run because the on/off switch is not working, the elements won't heat. If the motor runs but there is no heat coming out, the switch controlling the heating elements could be faulty. If neither element in a two-element dryer heats, check the overload protector before testing the element switch.

Switches often malfunction because they're dirty. If the motor doesn't run or the elements don't heat, clean the switches with electrical contact cleaner, as detailed above. If this doesn't solve the problem, and if the heating elements and the motor are not faulty, test the switches with a VOM, set to the R × 1 scale; the meter should read zero. If either switch is faulty, replace it with a new one made for the hair dryer. Connect the new switch the same way the old one was connected.

Hair Dryer Troubleshooting Chart

Caution: Disconnect power before inspecting or repairing.

PROBLEM	POSSIBLE CAUSE	SOLUTION
Hair dryer doesn't run	1. No power.	1. Check power cord, plug, and outlet. Check for blown fuse or tripped circuit breaker at main entrance panel; restore circuit.
	2. Power cord faulty.	2. Test cord; if faulty, replace.
	3. On/off switch dirty.	3. Clean on/off switch.
	4. On/off switch faulty.	4. Test on/off switch; if faulty, replace.
	5. Element switch dirty.	5. Clean element switch.
	6. Element switch faulty.	6. Test element switch; if faulty, replace.
	7. Motor faulty.	7. Take to a professional, or replace hair dryer.
Hair dryer shocks	1. Power cord faulty.	1. Test cord; if faulty, replace.
	2. Short circuit in electrical system.	2. Take to a professional.
Hair dryer heats but fan doesn't run	1. Fan dirty; fan needs lubrication.	1. Clean and lubricate fan.
	2. Motor shaft needs lubrication.	2. Lubricate motor shaft and bearing.
	3. Motor faulty.	3. Take to a professional, or replace hair dryer.
Fan runs but hair dryer doesn't heat	1. Element switch dirty.	1. Clean element switch.
	2. Element switch faulty.	2. Test element switch; if faulty, replace.
	3. On/off switch dirty.	3. Clean on/off switch.
	4. On/off switch faulty.	4. Test on/off switch; if faulty, replace.
	5. Overload protector faulty.	5. Test overload protector; if faulty, replace.
	6. Heating element faulty.	6. Replace heating element, or replace hair dryer.

Fan. If the dryer doesn't blow at all, or if it doesn't produce much hot air, the fan may be binding because of dirt or hair wound around the blades. Disassemble the dryer and clean the motor shaft and the bearing the fan turns on. Lubricate these parts with light household oil — sewing machine oil works well. Turn the fan by hand to test it. If it still doesn't turn easily, replace the fan with a new one made for the dryer. Remove the old fan by removing the bearing and pulling the fan off the motor shaft. Place the new fan on the motor shaft and connect it the same way the old one was connected; then replace the bearing.

If the fan is not binding, check the fan blades; they are made of metal or molded plastic. Metal fan blades may be bent; bend them gently back into shape with pliers. If the blades are severely bent, replace the fan, as detailed above. Plastic fan blades may break or melt; if the blades are damaged, replace the fan with a new one made for the hair dryer, as detailed above.

Motor. If the motor doesn't run, disassemble the hair dryer and turn the motor shaft by hand. If it's hard to turn, lubricate the shaft with light household oil — sewing machine oil works well. Turn the shaft again until it spins freely. Sometimes a hair dryer will run normally and then suddenly start to blow cold air; this is caused by a slow-turning motor. Dust and hair sucked into the air intake of the dryer can work their way into the motor bearing, slowing down the motor and causing it to overheat and shut off. Remove the fan and bearing, and clean the fan, the bearing, and the motor shaft. Then reassemble the parts.

If cleaning and lubrication don't start the motor, if it still won't turn by hand, or if it's hard to turn, take the dryer to an appliance repair outlet.

Mixers

Mixers are used to blend or mix ingredients in food preparation. Beaters driven by a universal motor do the work, and usually multiple mixing speeds are available, to fold, beat, or whip as needed. There are three styles of mixers in general use: hand-held, upright, and convertible. The upright mixers are the largest; they consist of a mixer mounted on a pedestal, which also supports the turntable the mixing bowl rests on. Hand-held and convertible mixers are smaller and lighter; there is little difference between them except that convertible models can be set on a pedestal or hand-held. All three types of mixers operate on the same principles.

Caution: Before doing any work on a mixer, make sure it is unplugged.

Cleaning and Lubrication. Most mixers have oil ports at the top of the motor assembly. Lubricate each port with a drop or two of heat-resistant oil every two to three months, or more often if the mixer is used frequently. Clean any food debris from the motor with a soft cloth; don't use abrasive paper. Once a year, clean the bearings and lubricate them with a drop of light-weight oil or sewing machine oil. Every 12 to 18 months, remove the retaining plate and clean the gears, as detailed below; then lubricate them with silicone gear grease.

Turntable. On most pedestal mixers, there is a small lever located under the turntable; this lever regulates the speed at which the turntable moves. If the lever is out of alignment, the turntable may stick in its mounting and fail to turn. Bend the lever slightly to realign it; if this doesn't work, take the mixer to an appliance repair outlet.

Beaters. If the turntable is working but the bowl doesn't turn, the beaters could be set too low, striking the bowl and slowing it down or stopping it completely. To adjust the beaters, tilt the housing up from the pedestal; locate the beater adjustment screw on top of the pedestal. Turn the screw clockwise to raise the beaters, counterclockwise to lower them.

If the beaters are bent or damaged, they cannot be repaired. Replace them with new beaters made for the mixer.

Gears. The gears are located directly above the beaters, and are held in place by a retaining plate. Unscrew the plate to get at the gears, and inspect the gears for worn or broken teeth. A broken tooth can produce a loud noise when the mixer is operating, or can cause one beater to stop turning. If a gear tooth is broken, replace both gears, even if only one is faulty; buy replacement gears made for the mixer.

To remove the old gears, pull them up and out of the mixer. If the gears don't pull right out, they are probably held by circlips where the beaters attach to the mixer; you will need a circlip pliers to release the circlips and remove the gears. Lubricate the new gears slightly with silicone gear grease before installing them. Most gears are marked with a dot or an arrow to facilitate correct placement; note the position of the mark on the old gears and set the new ones into place the same way. When the gears are in place, turn the motor shaft by hand. The gears should mesh. If they don't, reposition them and turn the motor shaft again. Repeat this procedure until the gears mesh smoothly.

Mixer Attachments. Mixer attachments such as coffee grinders, juicers, and ice crushers operate off gears similar to the beater gears. If trouble occurs with any of these attachments, check these gears for wear or breakage. The gears are located in the attachment itself; unscrew a cover plate to reach them. If the gears are worn or broken, replace them with new gears made for the attachment. Lift the old gears out of the attachment, and put the new gears into position. To keep the attachments working properly, clean the gears and lubricate them with silicone gear grease at least once a year.

Switch. The switch is located inside the mixer housing, and is usually mounted on a bracket attached to the ejector or gear retaining plate. If the motor doesn't run, and the problem is not in the power cord, the switch may be faulty; if the motor runs all the time, the switch is definitely faulty. Lack of power at only one speed can also be caused by a faulty, disconnected, or loose wire in the switch terminals. Check to make sure the switch connections are clean and tight. If the contacts are dirty or corroded, rub them gently with a fine emery board, and then with a soft cloth; if they're misaligned, bend them back into place. Tighten any loose terminal screws.

Switch malfunctions can be caused by dirt in the switch. To clean the switch, disconnect the lead wires to it and lift the switch out. Spray the terminals and the switch with electrical contact cleaner, available at appliance repair and electrical supply outlets. Flip the switch back and forth several times to work the cleaner into the moving parts; then wipe it clean with a soft cloth, and reinstall the switch.

If the switch contacts or terminals are badly corroded, if cleaning the contacts and the switch and tightening the terminals doesn't restore power to the mixer, or if there is no apparent problem with the switch contacts and terminals, replace the switch with a new one made for the mixer.

To replace the switch, remove the screws that hold the switch to the housing and disconnect the lead wires. If the leads have friction-fit plug connectors, use a long-nosed pliers to grip the plugs—don't pull them off with your fingers; you could break the wires. Connect the new switch the same way the old one was connected. If the switch is riveted to the housing, don't try to replace it yourself; take the mixer to an appliance repair outlet.

Switch replacement should solve most problems. If the motor still runs at only one speed after the switch is replaced, the speed governor may be faulty. In this case, take the mixer to an appliance repair outlet.

Fan. The fan is located at the rear of the motor. If the mixer is very noisy or vibrates excessively, the fan blades could be bent. If the blades are bent slightly, bend them back into their original position with a pliers. If bending is not possible, or if the blades are severely bent, replace the fan with a new one made to fit the mixer. The fan is held in position by a retaining bracket over its shaft; remove the screws that hold the bracket to remove the fan. Connect the new fan the same way

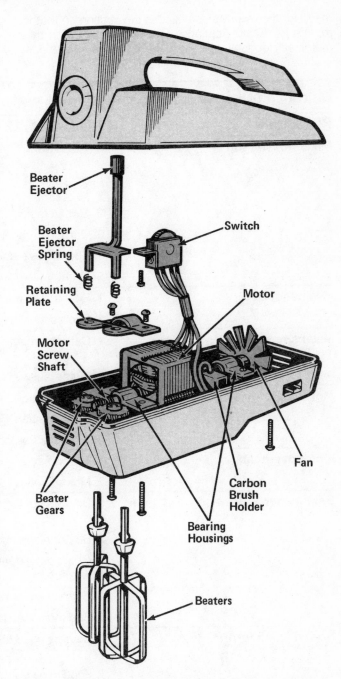

All mixers—hand-held, upright, and convertible units— use beaters driven by a universal motor. The gears are located directly above the beaters.

the old one was connected; then replace the bracket and screws.

Motor. If the switch has been repaired and the motor still doesn't run, or if it runs erratically, makes noise, smells, or sparks, the motor's carbon brushes are probably worn. Replace them with new carbon brushes made for the mixer, as detailed in the section on motor repairs in "Basic Appliance Repair Principles." If the motor still doesn't run, or if there are more serious motor problems — such as a faulty speed governor, loose armature windings, or shocking—take the mixer to an appliance repair outlet.

Mixer Troubleshooting Chart

Caution: Disconnect power before inspecting or repairing.

PROBLEM	POSSIBLE CAUSE	SOLUTION
Mixer doesn't run	1. No power.	1. Check power cord, plug, and outlet. Check for blown fuse or tripped circuit breaker at main entrance panel; restore circuit.
	2. Switch faulty.	2. Check switch; if faulty, replace.
	3. Carbon brushes worn.	3. Check brushes; if worn, replace.
	4. Speed governor faulty.	4. Take to a professional.
	5. Motor faulty.	5. Take to a professional.
Mixer shocks	1. Power cord faulty.	1. Test cord; if faulty, replace.
	2. Short circuit in electrical system.	2. Take to a professional.
Mixer sparks	1. Carbon brushes worn.	1. Check brushes; if worn, replace.
	2. Motor faulty.	2. Take to a professional.
Motor stuck on single speed	1. Switch or switch contacts dirty.	1. Clean switch or switch contacts.
	2. Switch faulty.	2. Replace switch.
	3. Speed governor faulty.	3. Take to a professional.
Motor overheats	1. Motor dirty.	1. Clean and lubricate motor.
	2. Motor faulty.	2. Take to a professional.
Beaters don't turn	1. Beaters not locked in unit.	1. Push beaters firmly into shafts until they are properly engaged.
	2. Beater blades bent.	2. Replace beaters.
	3. Gears dirty; gears need lubrication.	3. Clean and lubricate gears.
	4. Gears worn or damaged.	4. Replace gears.
	5. Bearings need lubrication.	5. Lubricate bearings.
Bowl doesn't turn	1. Beaters need adjusting.	1. Adjust beaters so they don't strike bowl.
	2. Food in bowl too thick.	2. Add more liquid to bowl.
	3. Control lever out of alignment.	3. Realign control lever, or take to a professional.
	4. Turntable assembly damaged.	4. Take to a professional.
Excessive vibration	1. Beaters need adjusting.	1. Adjust beaters so they don't strike bowl.
	2. Beater retaining plate loose.	2. Tighten retaining plate.
	3. Gears worn or damaged.	3. Replace gears.
	4. Fan blades bent.	4. Straighten fan blades, or replace fan.

Shavers

An electric shaver consists of a series of cutters on a movable head, driven by a motor. The head moves in a straight line or rotates under a thin, flexible metal head. Holes or slots in this head catch whiskers as the shaver moves, and the cutter clips them off. The key to trouble-free shaver use is cleaning after each shave, and light lubrication every month or so.

Caution: Before doing any work on a shaver, make sure it is unplugged.

Disassembly. Most shavers can be disassembled for cleaning; many can be disassembled via retaining screws for service. Opening the housing to get at the working parts of the shaver depends on the type of shaver; many shavers are sealed by the manufacturer, and can be serviced only by a professional. Because shavers, and their component parts, are so small, small tools are needed for repairs; regular size screwdrivers and pliers usually cannot be used.

To disassemble a rotary-head shaver, release the shaving head by removing the screws that hold the

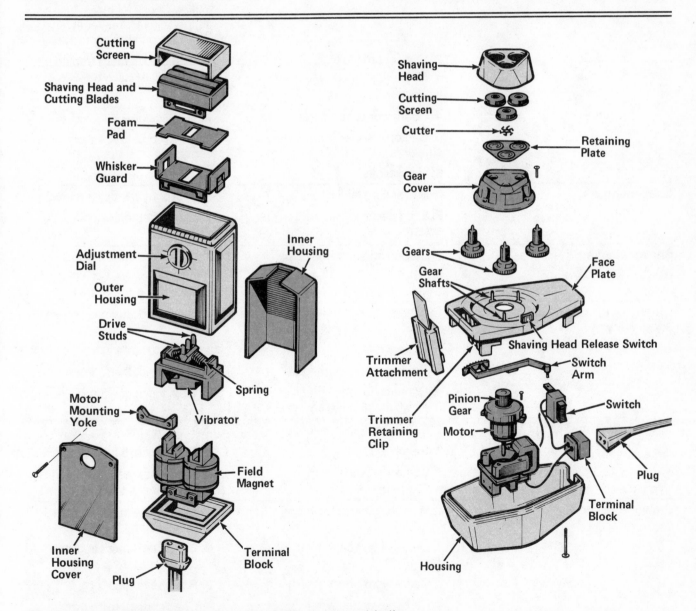

Flat- or curved-head shavers (left) have cutters that move in a straight line.
Rotary-head shavers (right) have cutters that rotate in a circle.

shaver in a clamshell configuration. If the shaver has a built-in trimmer attachment, remove the trimmer by pressing down on a spring clip and sliding the trimmer out of the housing. The gears are located behind a flat metal plate held in place by retaining screws. Remove the retaining screws to expose the gears; remove the gears for replacement or cleaning and lubrication by pulling them straight off their individual shafts. To take out the motor, switch, switch arm, and terminal block, remove the motor mounting screws.

To disassemble a curved-head shaver, remove the shaving head; you may have to set the dial to "clean." Then remove the cutting blades and the foam rubber pad they rest on. Turn the dial to the lowest setting. With the tip of a small screwdriver, separate the inner and outer housings; then remove the working parts of

Electric Shaver Troubleshooting Chart

Caution: Disconnect power before inspecting or repairing.

PROBLEM	POSSIBLE CAUSE	SOLUTION
Shaver doesn't run	1. No power.	1. Check power cord, plug, and outlet. Check for blown fuse or tripped circuit breaker at main entrance panel; restore circuit.
	2. Power cord faulty.	2. Test cord; if faulty, replace.
	3. Gears dirty; gears need lubrication.	3. Clean and lubricate gears.
	4. Gears worn or damaged.	4. Replace gears.
	5. Carbon brushes worn (rotary shavers).	5. Check brushes; if worn, replace.
	6. Motor faulty.	6. Take to a professional.
Shaver shocks	1. Power cord faulty.	1. Test cord; if faulty, replace.
	2. Short circuit in electrical system.	2. Take to a professional.
Shaver sparks	1. Carbon brushes worn. (rotary shaver).	1. Check brushes; if worn, replace.
	2. Motor faulty.	2. Take to a professional.
Cutters bind or don't cut adequately	1. Cutters need cleaning or lubrication.	1. Clean and lubricate cutters.
	2. Cutters dull.	2. Replace cutters.
	3. Cutting screen damaged.	3. Replace cutting screen.
	4. Connecting rods broken or bent (curved- or flat-head shavers).	4. Replace connecting rods.
Shaver starts and stops	1. Switch connections loose.	1. Tighten switch connections.
	2. Switch faulty.	2. Test switch; if faulty, replace.
	3. Carbon brushes worn (rotary shavers).	3. Check brushes; if worn, replace.
Shaver runs slowly	1. Voltage selector set wrong.	1. Set voltage selector to 110-volt setting.
	2. Gears dirty; gears need lubrication.	2. Clean and lubricate gears.
	3. Gears worn or damaged.	3. Replace gears.
	4. Carbon brushes worn (rotary shavers).	4. Check brushes; if worn, replace.

the shaver as a single unit. Remove the retaining screws on the inner housing, and remove this cover. Below the cover is a unit consisting of a vibrator and a field magnet; remove the screws that hold this unit.

To disassemble a flat-head shaver, set the dial to "clean," and remove the shaving head by pulling up on it. A foam pad usually separates the shaving head from the inner parts. Turn the dial to its lowest position, and pry the inner and outer housings apart with a screwdriver inserted near the adjustment control. Remove the inner body of the shaver. With the blade of a small knife, pry off the sides of the vibrator cover. Be careful not to damage or bend the whisker guards on the end of the cover. Remove the screws that hold the housing together in a clamshell configuration; this exposes the vibrator and field magnet units.

Cleaning and Lubrication. After each use, clean the shaver heads with the small brush provided by the manufacturer; or remove the shaving head and the cutters and wash them under running water. Dry the parts thoroughly; let them air-dry thoroughly before replacing them. Once a month, clean and oil the cutting blades with a light household oil—sewing machine oil works well.

Cutting Heads and Screens. If the shaver doesn't cut well, the cutting heads may be dull or the cutting screen damaged. If the blades are dull, replace them with new blades made for the shaver, or have them sharpened at an appliance repair outlet. Replace a damaged cutting screen with a new one.

Gears. Once a year, disassemble the shaver; clean the gears and lubricate them with light household oil. During this maintenance procedure, remove the gears, if possible, and check them for wear or damage. If a gear is worn or broken, replace it with a new gear made for the shaver. Install the new gear the same way the old one was installed.

Switch. If the shaver doesn't run, and the power cord is not faulty, the switch could be faulty. Remove the drive assembly and motor, disconnect the switch power leads, and remove the switch from the shaver. The leads are probably friction-fit; use long-nosed pliers to grip them. Do not try to disconnect the leads by hand; you could break the wires. Test the switch with a VOM, set to the R × 1 scale; the meter should read zero. If the switch is faulty, replace it with a new one made for the shaver. Connect the leads to the new switch and position it in the shaver the same way the old switch was installed; then reassemble the shaver.

Motor. If the motor runs slowly or sluggishly, make sure the voltage selector on the shaver is set to the 110-volt setting; the shaver will not run properly on the 220-volt setting.

Rotary-head shavers have universal motors; if the motor doesn't run or if it runs erratically, makes noise, smells, or sparks, the carbon brushes may be worn. Open the shaver to expose the motor. The brushes are located under a spring-loaded retainer on the motor. Release the brushes by prying the spring arm over and out from under a metal lip; remove the brushes by tipping the shaver over and tapping it. Replace the brushes with new ones made for the shaver, as detailed in the section on motor repairs in "Basic Appliance Repair Principles." For motor problems in a curved-head or flat-head shaver, take the shaver to an appliance repair outlet.

If the motor runs but the cutters don't work, the connecting rods that drive the blades could be broken or bent. These rods are usually found on curved-head and flat-head shavers. Spread the connecting rods open with a screwdriver and remove the tiny pins that hold the rods in position. Replace the rods with new ones made for the shaver; install the new rods the same way the old ones were installed.

If the motor seems to be jammed and the shaft won't turn, turn the pinion gear by hand. If this works, lubricate the bearings with light household oil — sewing machine oil works well. If this doesn't work, take the shaver to an appliance repair outlet.

Toaster Ovens

A toaster oven is, essentially, a smaller version of an electric range oven. The oven has a door that opens to expose a metal tray. Two or more heating elements, positioned below and above the cooking tray, are used; reflectors inside the toaster oven intensify the heat produced by the elements. The heating elements are controlled and regulated by a temperature control knob and a control switch. Opening the oven door turns the unit off automatically. Some toaster ovens have a timer for controlling the cooking period; others have a motor that turns a rotisserie attachment.

Caution: Before doing any work on a toaster oven, make sure it is unplugged.

Cleaning. The power terminals in a toaster oven accumulate grease and dirt, and this can cause trouble. At least once a year, disassemble the oven and clean the terminals; unhook each terminal and buff the metal lightly with very fine steel wool. This improves the electrical contact at the terminals. Use a soft cloth moistened with a solution of water and mild household detergent to clean any grease from the unit. Keep the reflecting panels inside the oven clean; buff them lightly to maintain heating and cooking efficiency. Clean the metal crumb tray at least once a month to keep the toaster oven free of debris.

Door. The door of the toaster oven can cause problems if it won't latch properly; the oven won't operate with the door open. If the door won't stay latched, the problem is probably in the latch and spring assembly. If the spring has slipped out of its holes, reconnect it. If the spring is badly stretched or broken, replace it with a new one of the same type; unhook the old spring and hook the new one into place. If the latch and latch release bind or won't catch, clean them thoroughly; then lubricate the latch and the latch release with heat-resistant lubricant, made for use in heat-producing appliances. If the door still doesn't latch properly, replace the latch with a new one made for the oven; tighten the door hinges or replace them with new ones. If necessary, replace the entire oven door with a new one made for the unit.

Heating Elements. The oven's heating elements may be either coiled resistance wires or rigid elements; they are either plugged or screwed into their terminals. If the elements don't heat, first check the connections and make sure the elements are firmly plugged or screwed in; tighten the screws or plug the elements in tightly. If the connections are good but an element still doesn't heat, it may be faulty. Test the heating element with a VOM. Unplug or unscrew the element from its terminals; in some toaster ovens you might have to disassemble the unit to do this. Clip the probes of the VOM to the element terminals, and set the meter to the R × 1 scale. If the VOM reads from 10 to 20, the element is in working order; if it reads higher than 20, the element is faulty, and should be replaced. Replace a faulty element with a new one made for the toaster oven; install the new element the same way the old one was installed.

Indicator Light. Toaster ovens sometimes have an indicator light, which goes on when the oven is turned on. If the indicator light doesn't go on, the bulb is probably burned out. Disassemble the oven as necessary to reach the indicator light, and disconnect the bulb. Replace the burned-out bulb with a new one of the same type and electrical rating, made for use in heat-producing appliances. Connect the new bulb the same way the old one was connected.

Setting Control Switch. The control switch on a toaster oven has several settings; if the oven does not heat, the problem could be with this switch. Remove the control panel and check the switch terminals; if they are dirty or corroded, clean them with very fine steel wool. If the oven still doesn't heat, the switch could be faulty. Test the switch with a VOM. Clip one probe of the tester to one of the switch terminals, and set the meter to the R × 1 scale. Then touch each

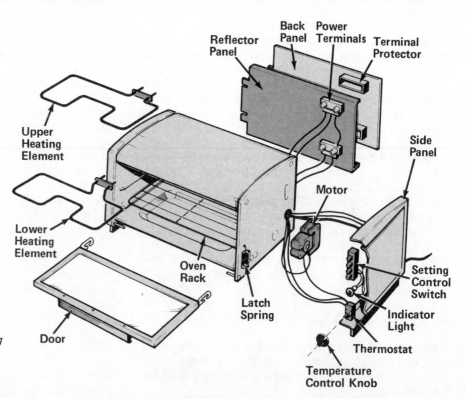

Toaster ovens use two or more heating elements controlled by a temperature control knob and a setting switch. Some toaster ovens have a timer for controlling the cooking period.

88

other terminal in turn with the other probe of the VOM. If the control switch is working properly, the VOM should read zero at each switch setting; if the meter reads higher than zero at any setting, the switch is faulty, and should be replaced. Replace the faulty control switch with a new switch made for the toaster oven. Disconnect the lead wires from the old switch, back out any screws holding the switch to the oven housing, and

Toaster Oven Troubleshooting Chart

Caution: Disconnect power before inspecting or repairing.

PROBLEM	POSSIBLE CAUSE	SOLUTION
Oven doesn't heat	1. No power.	1. Check power cord, plug, and outlet. Check for blown fuse or tripped circuit breaker at main entrance panel; restore circuit.
	2. Power cord faulty.	2. Test cord; if faulty, replace.
	3. Control switch set wrong.	3. Set control switch properly.
	4. Control switch faulty.	4. Test switch; if faulty, replace.
	5. Thermostat faulty.	5. Test thermostat; if faulty, replace.
	6. Timer faulty.	6. Have timer tested; if faulty, replace.
Oven shocks	1. Power cord faulty.	1. Test cord; if faulty, replace.
	2. Short circuit in electrical system.	2. Take to a professional.
Oven doesn't get hot enough	1. Control switch set wrong.	1. Set control switch properly.
	2. Thermostat needs adjusting.	2. Reset thermostat to higher temperature.
	3. Heating element faulty.	3. Test element; if faulty, replace.
	4. Timer faulty.	4. Have timer tested; if faulty, replace.
Oven gets too hot	1. Control switch set wrong.	1. Set control switch properly.
	2. Thermostat needs adjusting.	2. Reset thermostat to lower temperature.
	3. Timer faulty.	3. Have timer tested; if faulty, replace.
Door doesn't close	1. Latch spring disconnected or broken.	1. Reconnect or replace latch spring.
	2. Door latch needs lubrication.	2. Lubricate door latch.
	3. Door latch or hinges damaged.	3. Replace door latch or hinges.
Indicator light doesn't light	1. Bulb terminals dirty.	1. Clean bulb terminals.
	2. Bulb burned out.	2. Replace bulb.
	3. Heating element faulty.	3. Test element; if faulty, replace.
Rotisserie doesn't turn	1. Motor terminals loose or dirty.	1. Clean and tighten motor terminals.
	2. Gears dirty.	2. Clean gears.
	3. Gears worn or damaged.	3. Replace gears.
	4. Motor faulty.	4. Test motor; if faulty, replace.
	5. Short circuit in electrical system.	5. Take to a professional.

remove the old switch. Position the new switch in the unit and connect it the same way the old switch was connected.

Thermostat. A small bimetallic strip thermostat, regulated by a control knob, controls the amount of heat generated by the oven's heating elements. If the heating elements don't heat, and the control switch is functioning, check the contact points in the thermostat; if they are dirty or corroded, clean them with a fine emery board and a soft cloth. If the elements still don't heat, the thermostat could be faulty.

Test the thermostat with a VOM. Remove the lead wires from their terminals and set the control switch to high; clip the probes of the VOM to the thermostat terminals, and set the meter to the R × 1 scale. If the meter reads zero, the thermostat is working; if the meter reads higher than zero, the thermostat is faulty, and should be replaced. Replace a faulty thermostat with a new one made for the toaster oven. Remove the screws holding the thermostat to the oven housing and take the thermostat out. Position the new thermostat and install it the same way the old thermostat was installed, first screwing it to the oven housing and then connecting the terminals.

Timer. Some toaster ovens have a timer connected to the thermostat to turn the heating element on and off automatically at preset times. If the oven gets too hot, it could be because the timer isn't turning it off when it's supposed to; if the oven doesn't get hot enough, the timer could be turning the oven off too quickly.

The timer is located on the control panel; pull off the timer knob and other knobs and controls and remove the control panel to get at it. Check the timer's terminals; if the wire terminals are burned, dirty, or corroded, remove the leads and buff them and the terminal points with a fine emery board and a clean cloth. Then replace the leads and tighten all connections. If the timer still doesn't work properly, it's probably faulty.

Remove the timer and take it to an appliance repair outlet for testing; don't try to test it yourself. Make a diagram of the timer's connections so you'll be able to reconnect it properly; then disconnect all wires leading to the timer. Take out the screws or release the spring clips that hold the timer to the oven housing, and take out the timer. If the timer is faulty, replace it with a new one made for the toaster oven. Connect the new timer the same way the old one was connected.

Motor. If the toaster oven has a rotisserie, and it doesn't turn, either the gears are jammed or the motor has failed. Clean away any debris that might interfere with gear movement, and try turning each gear by hand. If the gears spin easily, the motor is probably faulty; if the gears won't spin or are very difficult to turn, the gears could be jammed or stripped. In this case, the gears should be replaced. In some toaster ovens the gears and motor are one assembly; if the gears fail the entire assembly — gears and motor — must be replaced. Replace the gears or the assembly with new gears or a gear-motor assembly made for the toaster oven. Remove the gears by taking out the mounting screws that hold the gear box; the whole assembly then lifts out. Set the new gear box or gear-motor assembly into position; make sure the gears are engaging the motor shaft. Then secure the screws that hold the assembly in place.

If the gears are not faulty, test the motor with a VOM. Disconnect the motor leads and clip the probes of the VOM to the leads. Set the meter to the R × 1 scale. If the meter reads between 40 and 100, the motor is functioning properly; if the meter reads higher than 100, the motor is faulty, and should be replaced. Replace the motor with a new one made for the toaster oven. Remove the screws that hold the motor to the oven housing, and remove the old motor. Set the new motor into place in the same position the old one was in, and replace the screws that hold the motor to the housing. Connect the motor leads the same way the old motor leads were connected.

Vacuum Cleaners

There are two types of vacuum cleaners—upright and canister or tank models. In both types, air is sucked through a sweeper assembly, past a fan, and into a dust bag; a universal motor provides the power. In upright vacuum cleaners, the same motor that runs the fan drives a beater bar assembly located in the nozzle of the unit; air is sucked in at the nozzle, moves over the motor, and is vented out through the exhaust. The exhaust empties into a porous dust bag, which lets the air out but keeps the dust in. In canister models, the exhaust is located at the base of the unit, and the dust bag is over the motor. Many canister vacuums have power attachments driven by a small auxiliary universal motor in the beater bar head.

Caution: Before doing any work on a vacuum cleaner, make sure it is unplugged.

Cleaning. The major complaint with vacuum cleaners is that they aren't producing enough suction; the major cause of the problem is clogging somewhere inside the unit. Overfilled dust bags, dirty filters, obstructed brushes, and a clogged hose can all contribute to reduced suction or pickup power. Check the dust bag periodically and empty or replace it when it's

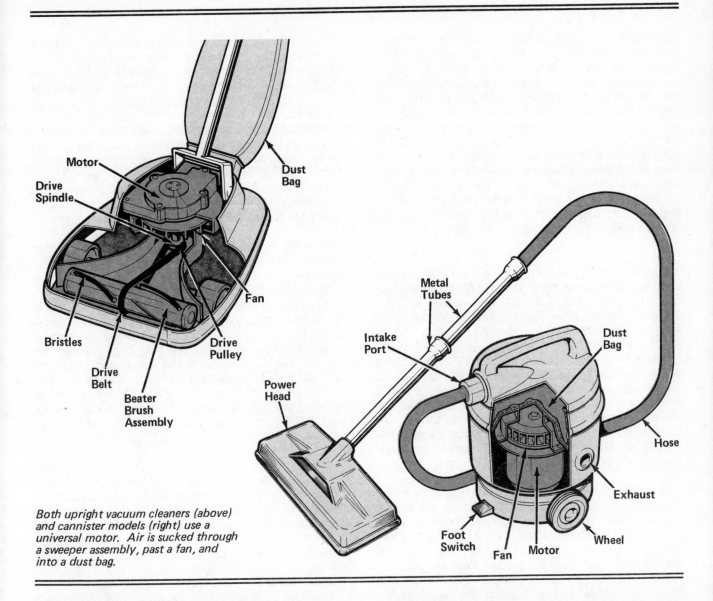

Both upright vacuum cleaners (above) and cannister models (right) use a universal motor. Air is sucked through a sweeper assembly, past a fan, and into a dust bag.

half to two-thirds full; a full dust bag cuts the vacuum's air flow. Determine your bag cleaning/changing schedule by the amount of vacuuming you do and the size of your living area; frequent vacuuming of large areas necessitates more frequent vacuum attention. If the motor is surrounded by a fiber filter, clean or replace this filter at least once a year. Slip the filter off the motor and wash it in a solution of water and mild household detergent; let it thoroughly dry before replacing it. Or replace it with a new filter made for the vacuum.

On upright vacuum cleaners and on the motor-driven attachments — power heads — of canister vacuums, carpet fibers, pieces of yarn or thread, hairs, and other long stringy debris often becomes wound around the beater brush assembly and the drive spindle. These obstructions can cause the drive belt to slip and prevent the beater brush from rotating. To solve the problem, turn the vacuum or the attachment over and remove the bottom plate.

Lift the dirt seal clamp at one or both ends of the brush and remove it; lift the brush and remove the drive belt to get the brush out. Wash the brush and fluff it with a coarse-toothed comb to restore it to its original effectiveness.

Power Cord. In canister vacuum cleaners with retractable power cords, dirt can get into the takeup reel and prevent the cord from retracting. This problem can usually be solved by cleaning. Remove the base of the canister by removing the screws on the side or on the underside of the base section; the reel is directly under the base. Clean all dirt, lint, and other obstacles from the reel. If the reel is still jammed, the rewind spring is probably faulty. In this case, take the vacuum to an appliance repair outlet.

Hose. If the vacuum cleaner hose is blocked— there's no suction when you place your hand over the nozzle—it must be cleaned. Disconnect the hose and use two straightened wire coat hangers, twisted together, to probe the hose. Push the coat hangers slowly through the hose, being careful not to damage it, and remove the obstruction. Then reconnect the hose.

Look for air leaks where the hose connects to the vacuum cleaner, and where the metal tubes of the handle slip together. The metal connection on the vacuum is usually screwed on; the connections from the hose to the metal tubes and between the metal tubes are push-fit. If these connections are bent open, pinch them together with a pliers to tighten the connection. If the parts are badly worn, or if they don't fit together firmly, replace them with new ones made to fit the vacuum.

Gasket. The gasket around the dust bag housing should be a tight seal; if the gasket is faulty, air will leak out around the housing, cutting down on the vacuum's suction. A hissing noise from this part of the vacuum is a sign of this problem. Remove the housing and inspect the gasket; look for loose or missing screws or loose spring clips around the gasket. Replace or tighten loose screws; tighten loose spring clips. If the gasket is hard, cracked, or broken, replace it with a new one made specifically for the vacuum cleaner. "Fit-all" gaskets may fit after a fashion, but tailoring them to fit the vacuum can be a tough job. Replace the gasket as detailed in the section on gaskets in "Basic Appliance Repair Principles."

Brushes. Upright vacuums and the power heads of canister vacuums can malfunction when the beater brushes become clogged. Clean the beater brushes thoroughly, as detailed above. When brushes become worn and the bristles don't extend past the bottom of the plate, they should be replaced. With the plate attached, hold a straightedge across each brush — a 3×5 card works fine — to check the length of the bristles. If the bristles do not extend past the bottom of the plate, replace the brush with a new one made to fit the vacuum. If the vacuum has two or more brushes, replace both of them at the same time.

If there is a suction problem and cleaning the brushes doesn't solve it, probe the passageway where the brush assembly connects to the vacuum. On an upright model, straighten a wire coat hanger and probe the passageways between the beater brush and the fan, and between the fan and the dust bag connection. On the power head of a canister unit, probe the connection between the brush head and the hose. Sometimes a passageway can be cleaned by removing the dust bag, or the hose connected to the power head, and turning the vacuum on to blow out any obstructions.

Drive Belt. The drive belt that turns the beater brush in an upright model or power head should be checked periodically to be sure it is in good condition. To check the belt, remove the unit's bottom plate. If the belt is stretched or cut, or if the brush doesn't rotate, replace the belt with a new one made for the vacuum. Note the way the old belt is positioned, and position the new belt the same way. To remove the belt, you'll have to take out the brush; lift up the dirt seal clamp, lift out the brush, and slide the old drive belt off the brush and the drive shaft. Stretch the new belt into place around the brush, and set the brush back into the vacuum. Use a screwdriver to stretch the belt end over the drive shaft. Check the brush and make sure it rotates freely; reposition the belt as necessary until it's properly aligned.

Wheels. Most vacuum cleaner wheels are plastic or metal. They are held to the housing with smooth-shanked bolts retained by nuts, or anchored to axles with spring clips. Remove the nuts and the bolts or pry the clips loose with a screwdriver or pliers. If a wheel is damaged, replace it immediately with a new wheel made for the vacuum—not only do the wheels make the vacuum easier to operate, they help maintain the level of the vacuum and the proper spacing between the bottom of the cleaner and the floor surface. A damaged wheel can cause problems with either level or spacing, causing the vacuum to operate less efficiently. Attach the new wheel the same way the old one was attached.

Switch. If the vacuum doesn't run and the power cord is not defective, the on/off switch is probably faulty. On upright vacuums, remove the switch plate on the handle by removing two screws. On canister vacuums, remove the topmost cover to reach the switch; turn the unit upside down and remove all visible screws from around the motor. Turn the unit right side up and lift up the cover. If the vacuum has a foot-operated switch, remove a pair of screws on the side or underside of the body to release the switch. Test the switch with a VOM, set to the R × 1 scale; the meter should read zero. If the switch is faulty, replace it with a new one made for the vacuum. Disconnect the lead wires to the switch; loosen the screws or pull off the friction-fit wires with long-nosed pliers. Connect the wires to the new switch the same way, and then fit the new switch into position and fasten it into place.

Fan. The fan of the vacuum cleaner is positioned on the shaft of the motor. If the fan becomes loose on the shaft, tighten the screw that holds it to the shaft. The screw may be in the hub of the fan or on the end of the motor shaft. If the fan blades look bent or worn, replace the fan blade assembly with a new one made for the vacuum. Straightening the blades is not recommended; the blades are specially engineered to create suction.

A small piece of debris — a pebble, a hairpin, or a matchstick—can become wedged between a fan blade

Vacuum Cleaner Troubleshooting Chart

Caution: Disconnect power before inspecting or repairing.

PROBLEM	POSSIBLE CAUSE	SOLUTION
Vacuum doesn't run	1. No power.	1. Check power cord, plug, and outlet. Check for blown fuse or tripped circuit breaker at main entrance panel; restore circuit.
	2. Switch faulty.	2. Test switch; if faulty, replace.
	3. Fan blades jammed.	3. Remove obstruction from blades.
	4. Carbon brushes worn.	4. Check brushes; if worn, replace.
	5. Motor faulty.	5. Take to a professional.
Vacuum shocks	1. Power cord faulty.	1. Test cord; if faulty, replace.
	2. Short circuit in electrical system.	2. Take to a professional.
Motor sparks	1. Carbon brushes worn.	1. Check brushes; if worn, replace.
	2. Motor faulty.	2. Take to a professional.
Little or no suction	1. Dust bag full.	1. Empty or replace dust bag.
	2. Dust bag not open.	2. Open bag by pulling out folds.
	3. Hose blocked.	3. Remove obstruction from hose.
	4. Hose not connected properly.	4. Make sure hose is properly seated in connecting port.
	5. Hose tubes loose or bent.	5. Tighten or replace hose tubes.
	6. Filter dirty.	6. Clean or replace filter.
	7. Screen dirty.	7. Clean screen.
	8. Fan loose.	8. Tighten fan on motor shaft; if blades are severely bent, replace fan assembly.
Nozzle or power head doesn't pick up	1. Nozzle obstructed.	1. Remove debris from beater brush and drive belt.
	2. Beater brushes worn.	2. Check brushes; if worn, replace.
	3. Drive belt worn or broken.	3. Replace drive belt.
Motor hums but doesn't run	1. Fan blocked.	1. Remove obstruction from blades.
	2. Short circuit in electrical system.	2. Take to a professional.
Motor starts and stops	1. Power cord not plugged in firmly.	1. Make sure plug is firmly seated in outlet.
	2. Power cord faulty.	2. Test cord; if faulty, replace.
	3. Switch connections loose.	3. Tighten switch connections.
	4. Carbon brushes worn.	4. Check brushes; if worn, replace.
	5. Motor faulty.	5. Take to a professional.
Motor runs too fast	1. Dust bag full.	1. Empty or replace dust bag.
	2. Hose blocked.	2. Remove obstruction from hose.
	3. Fan blades loose.	3. Tighten fan blades.
	4. Motor faulty.	4. Take to a professional.

and the housing and stop the motor. When this happens, the piece of debris sucked in will rattle around the housing and make a clanking noise; then the power will go off. To remove the obstruction, unplug the vacuum; then turn it upside down and rotate the fan blades by hand. On an upright unit, you'll have to remove the drive belt to do this. The obstruction should drop out. If this doesn't work, loosen the mounting bolts that hold the motor, and move the entire motor/fan assembly from side to side to remove the obstruction.

Motor. If the switch has been repaired and the motor still doesn't run, or if it runs erratically, makes noise, smells, or sparks, the motor's carbon brushes are probably worn. Replace them with new carbon brushes made for the vacuum, as detailed in the section on motor repairs in "Basic Appliance Repair Principles." If the motor still doesn't run, or if there are more serious motor problems, such as loose armature windings or shocking, take the vacuum cleaner to an appliance repair outlet.

Waffle Irons and Skillets

These two appliances are very similar in construction and in repair procedures. There is one major difference between them. Both contain a heating element, but the element in a skillet is sealed in the bottom of the pan, while the element in a waffle iron can be replaced. The heating element in a skillet seldom malfunctions, but when it does, repairs are not possible; the entire skillet must be replaced.

Caution: Before doing any work on a waffle iron or a skillet, make sure it is unplugged.

Heating Elements. In a skillet, the heating element is sealed in the bottom of the pan; if the element malfunctions, replace the entire skillet. In a waffle iron, the top and bottom heating elements are under the top and bottom grids; remove the grids to expose the elements. The top and bottom elements are connected with a hinge wire, which may be broken or loosely connected. Tighten the hinge wire connections; if the hinge wire is damaged, replace it with a new one made for the waffle iron. Remove the old wire, and connect the new wire the same way the old one was connected.

The heating elements in a waffle iron are coiled resistance-wire springs or enclosed elements, held in place in the top and bottom of the unit by ceramic fixtures. Examine the elements. If an element is broken or

sagging, it should be replaced; temporary repairs are possible, but they are not recommended. Replace a faulty element with a new one of the same type and electrical rating as the old one, preferably one made for the waffle iron. Unscrew the old element and remove it from the ceramic fixtures. Then position the new element on the fixtures and connect it the same way the old one was connected.

Waffle Iron Thermostat. In a waffle iron, the thermostat is located directly behind the control knob; to expose the thermostat, remove the grid. If the waffle iron doesn't heat or heats too slowly, the thermostat may be faulty. Disconnect the thermostat lead wires and test the thermostat with a VOM, set to the R × 1 scale; the meter should read zero. If the thermostat is faulty, replace it with a new one made for the waffle iron.

The control knob may be friction-fit on a shaft or may be held by a setscrew; pull the knob off the shaft, removing the setscrew if necessary. Remove the screws that hold the thermostat. If the thermostat is connected to a bracket clipped to the housing, gently pry out the clip and the thermostat with a screwdriver or pliers. If the thermostat is riveted or welded in place, don't try to replace it yourself; take the waffle iron to an appliance repair outlet.

After removing the old thermostat, install the new one. Connect the new thermostat the same way the old one was connected, and replace the mounting screws or clip to hold it in place.

Skillet Thermostat and Handle Unit. In a skillet, the thermostat is located inside the handle unit; to get at the thermostat, remove the screws that hold the handle together in a clamshell configuration, and open the handle. Or remove the plate on top of the handle to expose the working parts inside it. Then remove any aluminum foil covering the parts. Be sure to replace the foil when you reassemble the unit. Examine the thermostat contact points, near the base of the probe that plugs into the skillet. These points make contact when the skillet is turned on, and open when a preset temperature is reached or the skillet is turned off. If the contacts are dirty or corroded, rub them gently with a fine emery board, and wipe them clean with a soft cloth.

The handle unit of the skillet — the power probe — plugs into a terminal at the skillet base. Examine the terminal pins that stick out from the skillet base. If the terminals are loose, tighten the screws that attach them to the skillet. If the terminals look burned or pitted, replace them with new terminals made for the skillet. Remove the screw nuts that hold the terminals, insert the new terminals, and tighten the screw nuts securely.

If the skillet overheats, the problem may be that the thermostat contact points are fused together. If the contacts are fused, open them carefully with the tip of a

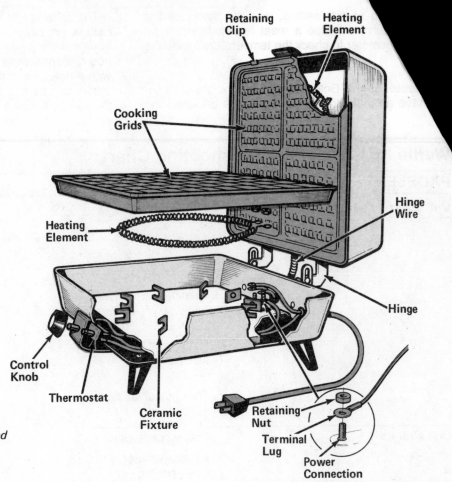

Retaining Clip

Heating Element

Cooking Grids

Heating Element

Hinge Wire

Hinge

Control Knob

Thermostat

Ceramic Fixture

Retaining Nut

Terminal Lug

Power Connection

The heating elements and electrical connections in a waffle iron are located beneath the grid plates. The heating elements are held in place by ceramic fixtures.

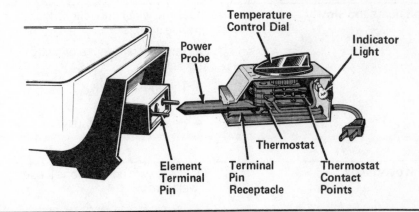

Temperature Control Dial

Power Probe

Indicator Light

Thermostat

Element Terminal Pin

Terminal Pin Receptacle

Thermostat Contact Points

An electric skillet is controlled by a thermostat contained in the handle unit, which plugs into the base of the skillet. The heating element is sealed in the base, and is not accessible.

screwdriver; smooth them gently with a fine emery board and then wipe them clean with a soft cloth. If the contacts are damaged, or if separating them causes damage, replace the thermostat with a new one made for the skillet. The thermostat may be held in place with screws or spring clips; remove the old thermostat and connect the new thermostat the same way the old one was connected. If the thermostat cannot be removed,

replace the entire handle unit with a new one made for the skillet.

On some skillets, the thermostat is adjustable. If the skillet does not reach the proper temperature, pry off the cap of the control dial to expose an adjustment screw in the center of the dial. Turn the screw slightly to recalibrate the control dial; you may have to experiment, turning the screw and then testing the tempera-

...til the thermostat is ...hermometer or an ...erature inside the

...e irons and skillets usu-...ght, which goes on when the unit is turned on. If the indicator light doesn't go on, the bulb is probably burned out. Disassemble the waffle iron or skillet as necessary to get at the indicator light, and disconnect the bulb. Replace the burned-out bulb with a new one of the same type and electrical rating, made for use in heat-producing appliances. Connect the new bulb the same way the old one was connected.

...ron/Skillet Troubleshooting Chart

Caution: *Disconnect power before inspecting or repairing.*

...OBLEM	POSSIBLE CAUSE	SOLUTION
Unit doesn't heat	1. No power.	1. Check power cord, plug, and outlet. Check for blown fuse or tripped circuit breaker at main entrance panel; restore circuit.
	2. Power cord faulty.	2. Test cord; if faulty, replace.
	3. Heating element faulty.	3. Replace heating element (waffle iron), or replace unit (skillet).
	4. Hinge wire loose or faulty (waffle iron).	4. Tighten hinge wire connections, or replace hinge wire.
	5. Thermostat faulty.	5. Test thermostat; if faulty, replace.
Unit shocks	1. Power cord faulty.	1. Test cord; if faulty, replace.
	2. Heating element touches housing (waffle iron).	2. Adjust or replace heating element.
	3. Short circuit in electrical system.	3. Take to a professional.
Unit heats too slowly	1. Hinge wire connections loose (waffle iron).	1. Tighten hinge wire connections.
	2. Terminal pins loose or faulty (skillet).	2. Tighten or replace terminal pins.
	3. Thermostat faulty.	3. Test thermostat; if faulty, replace.
	4. Heating element faulty.	4. Replace heating element (waffle iron), or replace unit (skillet).
Unit overheats	1. Hinge wire connections loose (waffle iron).	1. Tighten hinge wire connections.
	2. Terminal pins loose or faulty (skillet).	2. Tighten or replace terminal pins.
	3. Thermostat contacts fused (skillet).	3. Separate thermostat contacts, or replace thermostat.
	4. Thermostat faulty.	4. Test thermostat; if faulty, replace.
Indicator light doesn't light	1. Bulb connections loose.	1. Tighten bulb connections.
	2. Bulb burned out.	2. Replace bulb.